Abortion in India

Abortion in India
Myth and Reality

S.G. Kabra

RAWAT PUBLICATIONS
Jaipur • New Delhi • Bangalore • Hyderabad • Guwahati

ISBN 978-81-316-0564-6

Published by
Prem Rawat for **Rawat Publications**
Satyam Apts, Sector 3, Jawahar Nagar, Jaipur 302 004 (India)
Phone: 0141 265 1748 / 7006 Fax: 0141 265 1748
E-mail: info@rawatbooks.com
Website: www.rawatbooks.com

New Delhi Office
4858/24, Ansari Road, Daryaganj, New Delhi 110 002
Phone: 011 2326 3290

Also at *Bangalore, Hyderabad* and *Guwahati*

Typeset by Rawat Computers, Jaipur
Printed at Chaman Enterprises, New Delhi

Contents

Foreword

Dr S.G. Kabra, a pious soul, blends in him an ardent scholar, with professional excellence as a doctor, a researcher, a poet and a story writer. I have gone through his several publications in English, Hindi and in local languages, on any subject conceivable in medical field concerning humanism. This exhibits his commitment and dedication to the social causes he takes in hand.

The title he has chosen for his book *Abortion in India: Myth and Reality* by itself suggests that he intends to cover a long distance between myth and reality about the womb of a mother and for this, he has skilfully travelled the whole distance from conceiving to abortion and thereafter has handed over this classic which till date is unknown to a sizeable portion of population of this country.

The present book, which runs into about 200 pages, consists of nine chapters being a complete code, is apt for being prescribed in the curriculum in all faculties of the institutions where value-based education is imparted.

From the definition of abortion to the cruel use of tongs, the author has dealt with different methods of inducing abortion. This book is also an eye-opener from sociological point of view since it warns us about the future dangers from the side effect of the use/misuse of productions of the pharma world to causing the damage to basic fibre of the society due to growing imbalance in sex ratio. He has not only dealt with ethical sides but has also tried to educate the readers about the legal consequences of the violation of professional ethics of medical man/law man and for this he has included the substantial material in form of appendices in as much as 50 pages. The book is written in simple and lucid language, which can be understood by the students of any standard from a school to university.

I wish Dr Kabra himself translate this work in Hindi and also get it translated in regional languages and include some of the interesting stories he has written in his earlier books, as I am sure this book then would give a message to a large section of population of this country for which it is written.

I congratulate Dr Kabra for bringing out an excellent publication to serve the humanity.

Justice Vinod Shankar Dave

Acknowledgements

No work is ever really a product of a solitary scholar. While pursuing my work for the present book, I came across many people who helped me make this possible.

First of all, I am grateful to Justice Vinod Shankar Dave, former Judge, Rajasthan High Court for writing a very enlightening, encouraging and motivating foreword to this book. He has also been a source of inspiration for me ever since I started this work for which I am thankful to him. I also express my gratitude towards my medical colleagues – Dr Ramji Narayanan and Dr B.R. Madan — who have always encouraged me to write this book. Besides, my journalist friends – Sunny Sebastian, Abha Sharma and Rajendra Bora – have also helped me a lot in this endeavour. Mr K.K. Parnami has provided astute advice and professional assistance in editing the manuscript. I am thankful to them all.

Last but not least, my thanks are due to Shri Kailash Rawat and Shri Pranit Rawat, the publishers, without whose initiative, this book would not have seen the light of day.

1

What is Abortion?

Abortion, criminal abortion, medical termination of pregnancy, foeticide, female foeticide, foetal loss and female foetal loss are frequently used interchangeably creating confusion. The basic terms related to the subject, therefore, need to be defined to ensure parity.

Common Definitions of Abortion

- Abortion is the termination of pregnancy by any method (spontaneous or induced) before the foetus is sufficiently developed to survive independently (foetus less than 20 weeks of pregnancy).
- Another definition is the delivery of the baby/foetus that is less than 500 grams.
- Another (clinical) definition is the expulsion of the product of conceptus, spontaneous or induced, before viability.

Before considering the subject of abortion in detail, one should understand the terminology that is used in this context:

Conceptus: Is the product of conception itself, i.e., the result of the union of the sperm and ovum. The period of development of the conceptus from the time of conception is referred to as the gestation period and normally lasts 40 weeks.

Embryo: Is a conceptus less than 12 weeks old. An embryo has yet to acquire those features that allow it to be recognized as a human being.

Foetus: Is the conceptus in the later period of gestation (greater than 12 weeks) of pregnancy. At this stage, the conceptus can be recognized as human.

Viability: Refers to the chance for survival of a foetus outside the womb. A foetus is normally born when it is fully mature, at 40 weeks (i.e., term). However, it is theoretically viable after 28 weeks and when even if born after this period and before full maturity it may survive with expert neonatal intensive care. Since such care has progressed to a stage where a foetus of more than 20 weeks may be saved, in some countries the age of viability has been advanced to 20 weeks.

Miscarriage: Is the spontaneous expulsion of a foetus before viability. This is also called *spontaneous abortion.*

Premature birth: Is the expulsion of a viable foetus before term.

Medical termination of pregnancy (MTP): Is the termination of pregnancy on medical grounds, and is commonly referred to as *induced abortion.*

Foeticide: Means willfully and illegally causing death of an unborn conceptus (embryo, foetus or full-grown baby).

Female foeticide: Means willfully and illegally causing death of an unborn female conceptus.

Since the killing of a an embryo or foetus (of either sex) in the womb is a prerequisite step of medical termination of pregnancy, it follows that willful terminations within the ambit of the Medical Termination of Pregnancy Act up to 20 weeks of pregnancy, or the Indian Penal Code Section 312 at any stage of pregnancy, are not, strictly speaking, illegal and thus not considered 'foeticide'.

Foetal (pregnancy) loss (wastage): Refers to loss (death and expulsion) of a foetus by whatever means, or the death of the baby immediately after. It is indicator of the reproductive health of women. Female foetal loss is the selective loss of female foetus in the womb.

Abortion: Is the termination of pregnancy of a non-viable foetus by any method (spontaneous or induced). An alternative definition is the spontaneous or induced expulsion of a conceptus before its viability. For international acceptance, the period of viability has been brought down to 20 weeks or is deemed to be so in a foetus weighing less than 500 grams.

Criminal abortion: Refers to an illegally performed abortion, i.e., in contravention of the provisions of the Medical Termination of Pregnancy Act; or Section 312 and related sections of the Indian Penal Code. Thus, criminal abortions and foeticide are synonymous.

Types of Abortions

Abortion generally evokes an image of 'induced abortion', thereby overshadowing other causes of spontaneous foetal loss (pregnancy loss). Before briefly detailing these other causes, generally labelled as 'abortion', we will first discuss various types of abortion.

Abortions can be classified as either of the following:

1. *Spontaneous:* the process of expulsion of the product of conception (embryo, foetus, baby) occurs by itself (spontaneously).
2. *Induced:* some form of external intervention or interference (medicinal, physical or surgical) starts and completes the process of expulsion/extraction of the product of conception (embryo, foetus, baby).

Types of Spontaneous Abortion

1. *Threatened:* When a pregnant woman develops bleeding but the embryo/foetus is found on examination to be living.
2. *Inevitable:* When a pregnant woman vaginal bleeding and the embryo/foetus on examination is found to be already dead.
3. *Missed abortion:* When the dead products of conception are retained in the uterus for several weeks.
4. *Complete:* When the products of conception (embryo/foetus, membranes and placenta) are all expelled from the uterus.
5. *Incomplete:* When part of the product of conception remains inside the uterus (usually placenta) and the woman continues to bleed.

6. *Septic:* When infection of uterine cavity occurs during abortion.

Types of Induced Abortion

1. *Therapeutic:* When the continuation of pregnancy poses threat to the life of the mother and the abortion is done (induced) to save the life of the mother (see Section 312 IPC).
2. *Non-therapeutic:* When the continuation of pregnancy per se is not a threat to the life of the mother and the abortion is done for causes other than to save the life of the mother (see provisions of MTP Act).

Abortion in India

It is incorrect to say that causing abortion was illegal in India till the MTP Act came into force. Therapeutic abortion to save the life of mother was always legal. In India induced abortion or medical termination of pregnancy is permitted under Section 312 of the IPC and the Medical Termination of Pregnancy Act (MTP Act). Yet, of the 4 to 5 million abortions that take place annually in India, more than two-thirds of them are illegal and performed outside the statutory provisions of the MTP Act by untrained, unskilled persons and are performed under highly unhygienic conditions.

Under Section 45 (1860) of the Indian Penal Code, inducing abortion or causing "a woman with a child to miscarry" is a criminal offence, both for the physician who does it or the woman who procures it, except when it is done in "good faith to save the life of the woman". This, truly, is a therapeutic abortion. Thus, therapeutic abortion has been legal in India since 1860 when the continuation of pregnancy poses a threat to the life of the mother and if it is medically considered essential to terminate it to save the life of the mother. This was, and still is, a blanket provision for therapeutic abortion without any stipulations of who can do it, where it can be done or upto what stage of pregnancy it can be done. The only stipulation is that it has to be to 'save the life of the woman'. The same is now provided by Section 5 of the MTP Act.

2

Different Methods of Inducing Abortion

There are many methods of abortion. The procedure used depends largely upon the stage of pregnancy and the size of the unborn child. Dr J.C. Willke, in his book, *Abortion Questions and Answers* (Cincinnati: Hayes Publishing Co Inc., 1985), has categorised these methods into three groups:

- those that invade the uterus and kill the child by instruments, which enter the uterus through the cervix;
- those that kill the preborn child by administration of drugs and then induce labour and the delivery of a dead baby; and
- those that invade the uterus via an abdominal operation.

Dilation of the cervix is required in cervical methods of abortion. The usual method of dilation is to insert a series of instruments of increasing size into the cervix. A set of metal dilators are used to widen the cervix sufficiently to accommodate the instruments of abortion. In contrast with a normal birth, where this dilation occurs slowly over a period of many hours, the forceful stretching by the abortionist to widen the cervix takes seconds. This premature and unnatural stretching of the cervix can result in permanent physical injury to the mother. Laminaria (dehydrated material, usually seaweed) is sometimes used to reduce damage to the cervix. Inserted into the cervix the day before the scheduled abortion, it absorbs water and swells, gradually widening open the cervix in the process.

First Trimester Abortions (upto 12 weeks)

Surgical Methods

1. Menstrual regulation/aspiration (MR)
2. Dilation and suction curettage
3. Dilation and surgical curettage

Medical Methods

Abortion using injectable medication like methotrexate with misoprostol; or oral (abortion) pills mifepristone with misoprostol

Second Trimester Abortions (from 13 to 20 weeks)

Surgical Methods

Surgical evacuation: dilation and evacuation, aspirotomy, aspirotomy and hysterotomy.

Intra-amniotic instillation of drugs: hypertonic saline, urea, prostaglandins, and others.

Extra-ovular instillation of drugs: ethacridine lactate, hypertonic saline and prostaglandins.

Intra-uterine insertion of devices: bougies, catheters metreurynter.

Medical Methods

Extra-uterine methods: parenteral prostaglandins, and oxytocids.

What is it that is aborted? Are the tissues that are removed formless? Is there a recognizable living structure in the womb that is forcibly removed?

At 8–9 weeks the baby's eyelids begin to form and hair appears. By the ninth and tenth weeks the child in the womb sucks its thumb, turns somersaults, jumps, can squint to close out light, frowns, swallows, and moves its tongue.

At 12 weeks all arteries are present, including the coronary vessels of the heart. Blood circulates through these vessels to all parts of the body. The heart beat ranges during this foetal period from 110 to 160 beats per minute. All blood cells are produced by the liver and spleen, a job soon taken over by the bone marrow. White blood cells, important for immunity, are formed in the lymph nodes and thymus. Vocal cords are complete, and the child can and does sometimes cry (silently). The brain is fully formed, and the child can feel pain. The eyelids now cover the eyes, and will remain shut until the seventh month to protect the delicate optic nerve fibres.

At 14 weeks muscles lengthen and become organized. The mother will soon start feeling the first flutters of the baby kicking and moving inside her.

At 15 weeks the foetus has an adult's taste buds and may be able to savour the mother's meals if it could.

At 16 weeks though the foetus is about 18 cm long and weighs 200 gm, eyebrows, eyelashes and fine hair appear. The child can grasp with his/her hands.

At 18 weeks the foetus is now about 25 cm long. The child blinks, grasps, and moves its mouth. More hair grows on his/her head and body.

At 20 weeks the baby can hear and recognize his/her mother's voice. Though still small and fragile, the baby is growing rapidly and could possibly survive if born at this stage. Fingernails and fingerprints appear. Sex organs are visible. Using an ultrasound device, the doctor can tell if the child is a girl or a boy.

At 24 weeks the unborn child is covered with a fine, downy hair called lunago. Its tender skin is protected by a waxy substance called vernix. Some of this substance will still be on the child's skin at birth following which it will be quickly absorbed. The child practices breathing by inhaling amniotic fluid into his/her tender lungs.

At 30 weeks the umbilical cord is the baby's lifeline to the mother. In fact, it has been so for several weeks now. Nourishment is transferred from the mother's blood, through the placenta, and into the umbilical cord to the foetus. If the mother ingests any toxic substances, such as drugs or alcohol, the baby receives these as well.

At 32 weeks, the foetus sleeps 90–95 per cent of the day, and sometimes experiences rapid eye movement (REM) sleep, indicating that it can dream.

At forty weeks, the baby, now approximately 3 kg, is ready for life outside its mother's womb. At birth the placenta will detach from the uterus and the umbilical cord will cease to work as the child takes his first breaths of air. The child's breathing will trigger changes in the circulatory system and force all impure blood to now travel through the lungs for oxygenation.

Abortion Techniques in Some Detail

It must be realised that different methods are used under different circumstances and depend on the stage of development of the conceptus. No method of abortion is 100 per cent safe, and no method is 100 per cent successful.

Menstrual Extraction/Menstrual Regulation (MR)

This technique is used in the first eight weeks. At this early stage of development, suction abortions are performed using a smaller tube, requiring little dilation of the cervix. This is called "menstrual extraction". However, if all the foetal remains are not removed, infection results, requiring full dilation of the cervix and a scraping out of the womb.

Suction Aspiration

This is the most common method of abortion during the first 12 weeks of pregnancy. General or local anaesthesia is given to the mother and her cervix is quickly dilated. A suction curette (hollow tube with a knife-edged tip) is inserted into the womb. This instrument is then connected to a vacuum machine by a transparent tube. The vacuum suction, 29 times more powerful than a household vacuum cleaner, tears the foetus and placenta into small pieces which are sucked through the tube into a bottle and discarded.

Salt Poisoning (Saline Injection)

Used after 16 weeks (four months) when enough fluid has accumulated. A long needle is passed through the mother's abdomen into the baby's amniotic sac and a concentrated salt solution is injected. The baby normally drinks amniotic fluid, which he/she swallows as well and is poisoned by it. It also acts as a corrosive, burning off the outer layer of the baby's skin. It takes somewhat over an hour for the baby to begin dying from this method. Within 24 hours, labour will usually set in and the mother will give birth to a dead or dying baby. There have been many cases of these babies being born alive. They are usually left unattended to die. However, a few have survived and have later been adopted.

In India, medical termination of pregnancy under the MTP Act is permitted only upto 20 weeks of pregnancy. However, when continuation of pregnancy threatens the life of the mother, it may be terminated under Section 312 of the MTP Act at any stage.

Prostaglandin Chemical Abortion

This form of abortion uses chemicals developed by the Upjohn Pharmaceutical Co., which cause the uterus to contract intensely, pushing out the developing baby. The contractions are more violent than normal, natural contractions, so the unborn baby is frequently killed by them: some have even been decapitated. Many, however, have also been born alive.

Partial Birth Abortion

This procedure is accomplished in five steps as under:

1. Guided by ultrasound, the abortionist grabs the baby's legs with forceps.

2. The baby's legs are pulled out into the birth canal.
3. The abortionist delivers the baby entirely except for the head
4. The abortionist jams scissors into the baby's skull. The scissors are then opened to enlarge the skull.

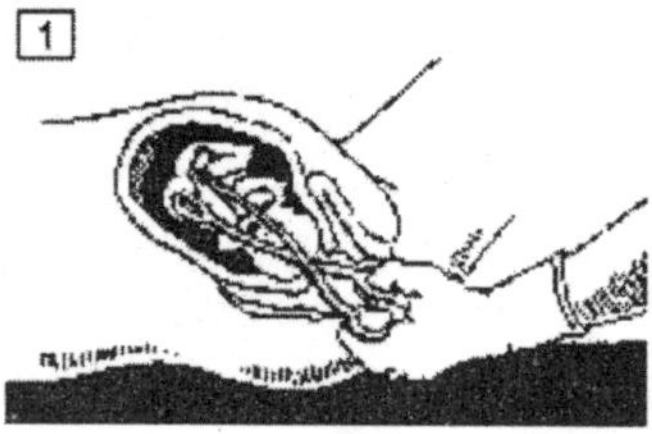

Guided by ultrasound, the abortionist grabs the baby's leg with forceps.

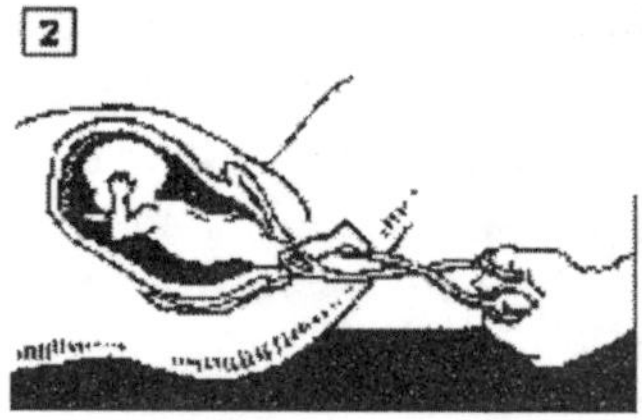

The baby's leg is pulled out into the birth canal

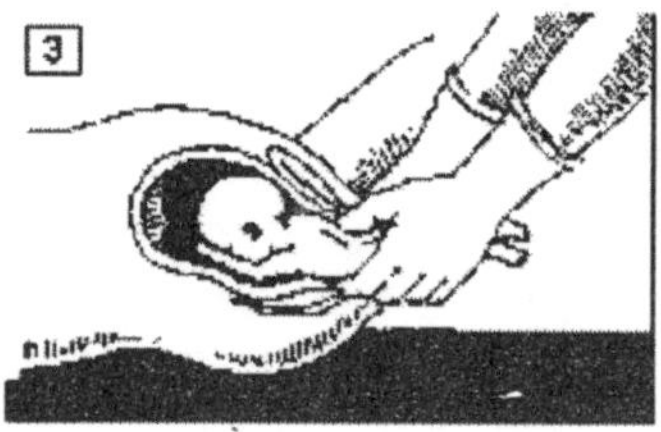

The abortionist delivers the baby's entire body, except for the head.

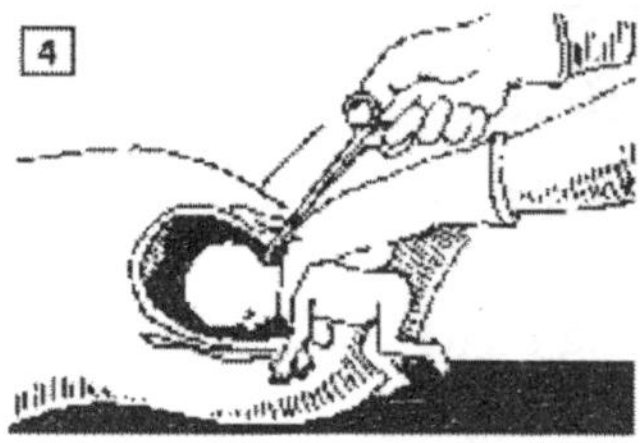

The abortionist jams scissors into the baby's skull. The scissors are then opened to enlarge the hole.

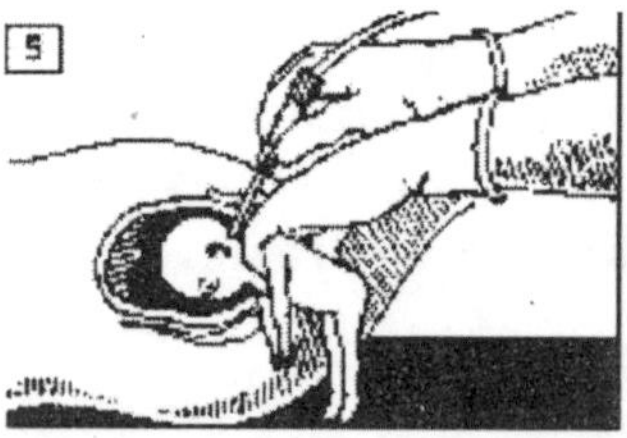

The scissors are removed and a suction tube is inserted. The child's brains are sucked out causing the skull to collapse. The dead baby is then removed.

5. The scissors are removed and a suction catheter is inserted. The child's brain is sucked out, causing the skull to collapse. The dead baby is then removed.

Methotrexate Injection

Performed in the early first trimester. Methotrexate is injected which begins to attack the cells surrounding the embryo. The embryo is deprived of food and oxygen and eventually dies. Several days later, misoprostol is injected to trigger the expulsion of the embryo. This expulsion may not occur for as long as eight weeks, and the woman may bleed heavily. The actual expulsion may occur at any moment and in any place. In about 4 per cent of cases, expulsion does not occur and surgery is required.

This is not a common form of abortion because Methotrexate is toxic and has many common side effects to the mother, such as nausea, pain, diarrhoea, and an increased chance of cancer, anaemia, and lung disease.

Suction Aspiration (Vacuum Curettage)

The most common (98%) form of first trimester abortion. The cervix is dilated, and a powerful vacuum tube with a sharp cutting edge is inserted. The suction rips apart the body of the baby, and sucks out blood, amniotic fluid, tissue, and body parts. The most frequent post-abortion complication occurs with this method. If any foetal or placental tissue is left behind in the uterus, infection can develop.

Dilation and Curettage (D&C)

This is generally performed in the first or early second trimester. The cervix is dilated or stretched to permit the insertion of a loop shaped steel knife. The body of the foetus is cut up and removed from the placenta. Blood loss and likelihood of uterine perforation are relatively high in this form of abortion.

This method is similar to the suction method with the added insertion of a hook shaped knife (curette) which cuts the baby into pieces. The pieces are scraped out through the cervix and discarded. This abortion method should not be confused with a therapeutic D&C done for reasons other than pregnancy.

Dilation and Evacuation (D&E) (Aspirotomy)

Generally performed in the second trimester, this is similar to D&C. Forceps are used to rip away pieces of the developing body and remove them from the womb. Because the skull has often hardened by this time, it may have to be crushed for removal. Bone fragments from the crushed skull can easily puncture the cervix, causing significant blood loss.

This method is used up to 18 weeks' gestation. Instead of the loop-shaped knife used in D&C abortions, a pair of forceps is inserted into the womb to grasp part of the foetus. The teeth of the forceps twist and tear the bones of the unborn child. This process is repeated until the foetus is totally dismembered and removed. Usually, the spine must be snapped and the skull crushed in order to remove them.

For some authors this method is known as 'aspirotomy' and is used where amniotic fluid is evacuated by suction before foetal parts are evacuated.

Prostaglandins Injection

This technique is used in the second trimester. Prostaglandins, naturally occurring birthing hormones, are injected to prematurely induce labour. Often the baby is delivered alive. Permanent placental, cervical, and cardiovascular side effects are common. Even death is possible.

Saline Amniocentesis (Salt Poisoning)

This method, first used in Nazi concentration camps and now common in the USA, is performed during the second or early third trimester. A needle is injected into the abdomen, and 50–250 ml of amniotic liquid is removed. This is replaced by a concentrated salt solution that corrodes the baby's skin. Within three days the mother goes into labour and delivers a dead, burned baby. This concentrated salt may cause severe haemorrhage, cervical injuries, seizures or coma in the mother.

Urea Injection

This is performed during the second or early third trimester and the method is similar to injecting a salt solution. Although not as strong or dangerous as salt, performed just like salt poisoning urea injection increases the chance of a failed abortion, which usually results in surgery. Almost 2 per cent of urea injection patients need hospitalization for side-effects.

Hysterotomy

Performed during the third trimester, this is usually performed if other forms of abortion are unsuccessful. Incisions are made in the abdomen, and the baby, placenta, and amniotic sac are removed. Babies are often removed alive during the operation. The risk to the mother's health is the greatest in this form of abortion, and the chance of complications during later pregnancies is greatly increased.

The technique is similar to a caesarean delivery, except that the umbilical cord is usually cut while the baby is still in the womb, thus cutting off his/her oxygen supply and causing it to suffocate. Sometimes, the baby is removed alive and simply left neglected in a corner to die of exposure.

Are these Methods Painful to the Foetus?

"Dilation and evacuation, for example, where foetal tissue is progressively punctured, ripped and crushed, and which is done after 13 weeks when the foetus certainly responds to noxious stimuli, would cause organic pain in the foetus, saline amnioinfusion, where a highly concentrated salt solution burns away the outer skin of the foetus, also qualifies as a noxious (painful) stimulus," said T. Sullivan, MD, FAAP of American Academy of Neurosurgeons.

Non-Therapeutic Second Trimester Termination of Pregnancies is Gross Human Rights Violation

On the occasion of signing the Partial Birth Abortion Act, 2003 on November 5, 2003, President Bush stated, "For years, a terrible form of violence has been directed against children who are inches from birth, while the law looked the other way. Today, at last, the American people and our government have confronted the violence and come to the defense of the innocent child."

It may be noted that the implied distinction between infanticide and partial birth abortion is "children who are inches from birth".

Alluding to the compelling evidence that led the members of the House and Senate to pass the legislation, President Bush stated: "The best case against partial birth abortion is a simple description of what happens and to whom it happens. It involves the partial delivery of a live boy or girl, and a sudden, violent end of that life. Our nation owes its children a different and better welcome."

A parallel second trimester termination of pregnancy permitted by law upto the 20th week of pregnancy and practised in India is Dilation and Evacuation (D&E). A medical doctor (Dr Tony Levatino, M.D.) who practised the procedure for long describes it in graphic detail:

"Imagine for a moment that you are a 'pro-choice' obstetrician-gynecologist as I once was. Your patient today is seventeen years old and she is twenty weeks pregnant. At twenty weeks, her uterus is up to her umbilicus and she has been feeling her baby kick for the last two weeks. If you could see her baby, she would be as long as your hand from the top of her head to the bottom of her rump not counting the legs. Your patient is now asleep on an operating room table with her legs in stirrups. Upon entering the room after scrubbing, you dry your hands with a sterile towel and are gowned and gloved by the scrub nurse.

"The first task is remove the laminaria that had earlier been placed in the cervix to dilate it sufficiently to allow the procedure you are about to perform. With that accomplished, direct your attention to the surgical instruments arranged on a small table to your right. The first instrument you reach for is a 14-French suction catheter. It is clear plastic and about nine inches long. It has a bore through the centre approximately three-fourth of an inch in diameter. Picture yourself introducing the catheter through the cervix and instructing the circulating nurse to turn on the suction machine which is connected through clear plastic tubing to the catheter. What you will see is a pale yellow fluid the looks a lot like urine coming through the catheter into a glass bottle on the suction machine. This amniotic fluid surrounded the baby to protect her.

"With suction complete, look for your Sopher clamp. This instrument is about thirteen inches long and made of stainless steel. At one end are located jaws about two-and-a-half inches long and about three-fourth of an inch wide with rows of sharp ridges or teeth. This instrument is for grasping and crushing tissue. When it gets hold of something, it does not let go.

"A second trimester D&E abortion is a blind procedure. The baby can be in any orientation or position inside the uterus. Picture yourself reaching in with the Sopher clamp and grasping anything you can. At twenty weeks gestation, the uterus is thin and soft so be careful not to perforate or puncture the walls. Once you have grasped something inside, squeeze on the clamp to set the jaws and pull hard – really hard. You feel something let go and out pops a fully formed leg about 4 to 5 inches long. Reach in again and grasp whatever you can. Set the jaw and pull really hard once again and out pops an arm about the same length. Reach in again and again with that clamp and tear out the spine, intestines, heart and lungs.

"The toughest part of a D&E abortion is extracting the baby's head. The head of a baby that age is about the size of a plum and is now free floating inside the uterine cavity. You can be pretty sure you have hold of it if the Sopher clamp is spread about as far as your fingers will allow. You will know you have it right when you crush down on the clamp and see a pure white gelatinous material issue from the cervix. That was the baby's brains. You can then extract the skull pieces. If you have a really bad day like I often did, a little face may come out and stare back at you.

"Congratulations! You have just successfully performed a suction D&E abortion. You just affirmed her right to choose. You just made 1600 cash in fifteen minutes".

For more medical information on D&E abortion: (i) *Abortion Practice,* by Warren M. Hern, M.D., M.P.H. (1990: Alpenglo Graphics, Inc., 1130 Alpine, Boulder, CO 80304); and (ii) *Second Trimester Abortion: Perspectives After a Decade of Experience,* edited by Gary S. Berger, William E. Brenner and Louis G. Keith (1981: Martinus Nijhoff Publishers, PO Box 566, 2501 CN The Hague, The Netherlands *and* John Wright, PSG, Inc., 545 Great Road, Littleton, MA 01460).

A pictorial presentation of D&E procedure is reproduced below to visualize and understand the same:

Dilation and Evacuation Abortion (D&E) of a 23-Week-Old Foetus

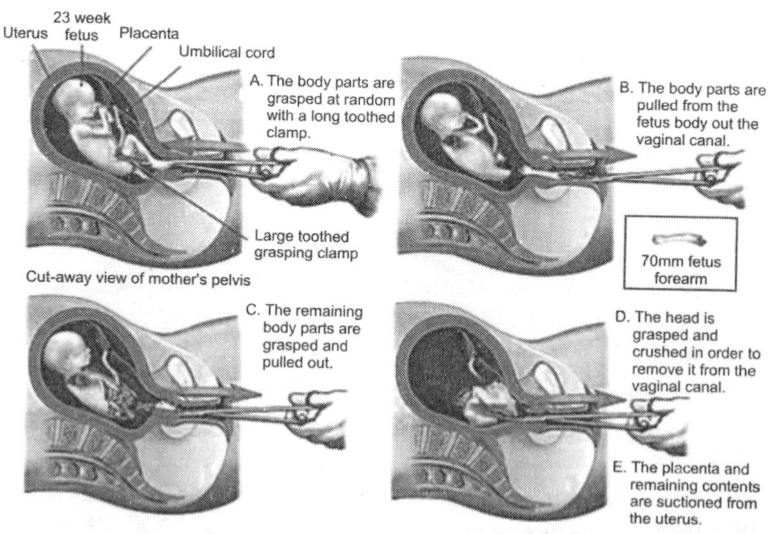

Obviously, an obstetrician or other physician who is required to, or opts to do the aforesaid procedures has to be desensitized to the tender feelings one expects for a tender life in the womb. One has to be totally indifferent, if not callous, to the life in the womb. Over enthusiastic and zealous abortionists are likely to be totally dehumanized.

Of the total of 96,79,484 registered Medical Terminations of Pregnancy done and reported since the MTP Act came into being, in a period from 1977 to 1997, 13 lakh 39 thousand, i.e., approximately 14 per cent were performed for second trimester abortion. Presently it is estimated that 40 to 50 lakh pregnancy terminations, registered and reported, unreported and clandestine, are being done in the country every year. All methods for second trimester abortion cause violent death of the live child in the womb.

Second Trimester Abortion

Comments

Dr B.R. Madan, Retired Professor and Head, Department of Pharmacology, Sardar Patel Medical College, Bikaner.

"If one reads the details of this procedure, as I have read, one is shocked that doctors who are supposed to personify nobility, compassion and empathy, can be so cruel and inhuman terminators of life. Perpetuation of this brutality against those who have a right to live, as much as you and I have, is an unforgivable crime. To condone or ignore this barbaric act is equally unforgivable."

Ms Abha Sharma, Journalist, Deccan Herald

"The procedure explained here about the second trimester abortions is horrifying. Medical science should serve as a great help to humanity and the rights of an unborn child should be protected at any cost. Necessary changes in the law and inculcating more ethical values in obstetricians can prevent merciless killings of innocent foetuses, mostly females."

"It is quite inhuman and unjust to allow abortions in the second trimesters and all stringent measures should be taken to stop this practice. It would be good if no termination of pregnancy is allowed in the second trimesters on the pretext of promoting family planning."

Mr Vinod Menon, Journalist, UNI, Jaipur

"I read your appeal to the RHRC. You've raised a very pertinent moral and ethical question. Thankfully, my mail did not contain pictures. When is the RHRC expected to reply to this? I shall circulate this in the hope it generates a wider public debate. Should you not send a copy to the President's website and to the Union Health Minister also?"

Mr Ramkant Rai, Health Watch, Lucknow

"It is nice to see such an important issue taken for advocating. It needs to be protested. I am afraid the feminist organizations will have some reservations. Hence, it needs to be discussed in some fora. I am with your view. Please keep us updated with your initiative."

Brigadier S.K. Puri, Faculty, IIHMR, Jaipur

"One really gets shivers after reading the whole text. I feel the Act needs to be reviewed and contraceptive failure abortions should be permitted upto 12 weeks and upto 20 weeks under IPC if the life of mother is threatened."

Dr Ramji Narayanan, Consultant Surgeon, SDM Hospital, Jaipur

"I did not realise that this procedure is so commonly performed in our country. It is obvious that the lacuna in the MTP Act that allows 2nd trimester abortions to be carried out with such impunity needs to be plugged. Otherwise, the numbers of this brutal operation will only increase. All surgical procedures are associated with a finite risk and a 2nd trimester abortion is no exception. When it is not medically indicated, it seems irrational and indeed dangerous to carry it out at all.

I hope the saner minds among our medical fraternity and legislators will prevail."

3

MTP Act: Mandatory Stipulations and Safety Provisions

The MTP Act has liberalized the availability of abortion by extending it when the pregnancy is likely to cause grave mental or physical injury to the mother and by including rape-induced and contraceptive-failure-caused pregnancies under it. However, this is permitted under strict statutory stipulations of supervised safety and responsibility. Indifference to the statutory stipulations of supervision, surveillance and monitoring by the designated health authority has rendered the law an excuse for illegal and criminal abortions by default. It is compounded by the pro-abortion lobby and the population control lobby's efforts to propagate abortion without insistence on implementation of the provisions of the MTP Act, and the regulation and the rules framed under it.

The Medical Termination of Pregnancy Act was enacted by the Indian Parliament in 1971 and came into force on 1st April 1972. The Act was revised in 1975 and amended in 2002. The Act lays down the conditions under which a pregnancy can be terminated, the persons who can perform it and the place where it can be performed. The provisions of the MTP Act are to be implemented, monitored and supervised by the Chief Medical Officer of the district, by whatever name he may be called, under the Medical Termination of Pregnancy

Regulations (2003) and the Medical Termination of Pregnancy Rules (2003).

The MTP Act has enlarged the scope of legal abortion and made safe abortion available to women up to 20 weeks of pregnancy under strict regulations and rules to ensure safety and to prevent its misuse.

Mandatory Stipulations of the Act

- the conditions (indications) for which abortion is permissible,
- the medical certification after which it can be done,
- the requirements of the centres where it can be done,
- the qualifications and competence of doctors who can do it, and
- the mandatory rules and regulations to be followed for doing it under the supervision of the Chief Medical Officer of the district.

Conditions for which Abortion can be done under the MTP Act

Under the MTP Act, an abortion may be carried out where

- the continuance of pregnancy involves risk to the life of the pregnant woman [Section 3(2)(i) of the MTP Act (see Section 312 IPC "to save the life of the woman")];
- the continuance of pregnancy involves grave injury to her physical or mental health [Section 3(2)(i), read with Section 3(3) of the MTP Act];
- there is substantial risk that if the child were born, it would suffer from such physical or mental abnormalities as would seriously handicap it [Section 3(2)(ii) of the MTP Act];
- any pregnancy is alleged by the pregnant woman to have been caused by rape [Explanation 1 Section 3(2) of the MTP Act]; and
- any pregnancy occurs as a result of failure of any (contraceptive) device or method used by any pregnant married

woman or her husband for the purpose of limiting the number of children [Explanation 2 under Section 3(2), read with Section 3(3) of the MTP Act].

Note: For rape-induced pregnancy, Explanation 1 Section 3(2) of the MTP Act stipulates that "the anguish caused by such pregnancy *shall* be presumed to constitute grave injury", but, for contraceptive failure, Explanation 2 Section 3(2) of the MTP Act stipulates that "anguish caused by such unwanted pregnancy *may* be presumed to constitute a grave injury" which in turn is further subject to determination/verification under Section 3(3) of the MTP Act by the certifying gynaecologist.

Mandatory Medical Certification after which Abortion can be Done

Medical certification is required before an abortion can be carried out. This certification may be granted by one medical practitioner if the length of pregnancy does not exceed 12 weeks [Section 3(2)(a) of the Act], but where the length of pregnancy exceeds 12 weeks (but does not exceed 20 Weeks), two registered medical practitioners [Section 3(2)(b)] will be required to grant certification.

The certification (MTP Regulation 3 in the Form I attached) must state that the practitioner/s is/are of opinion formed in good faith that the termination of pregnancy is necessary for one of the five stipulated indications in Section 3(2)(i), 2(ii), Explanation 1 or 2. The practitioner who then does the termination must certify within three hours of such termination the fact of such termination in Form I, and keep it in safe custody in a sealed and labelled envelope as per MTP Regulation 4(1–7).

Place where Pregnancy may be Terminated

An abortion may only be performed in a hospital established or maintained by the Government or at a place for the time being approved for the purpose of this Act by the Government or district level committee constituted by the Government (Section 4 MTP Act read with MTP Rules 3–7).

Note: Approval criteria where only first trimester abortions (<12 weeks) can be done are different from those where second trimester abortions are permitted (MTP Rule 5 (1)).

Doctors who can Terminate a Pregnancy

Under the MTP Act, a pregnancy can be terminated by a Registered Medical Practitioner who possesses recognized qualifications Under the Medical Council of India (MCI) Act; who is registered with a State Medical Council [Section 2(d) MTP Act]; and who has three years experience in the practice of gynaecology and obstetrics if registered before 1972 or who has worked as house surgeon for six months in Gynaecology and Obstetrics or who has a postgraduate degree or diploma in Gynaecology and Obstetrics or who is trained in medical termination of pregnancy through having assisted in 25 such procedures terminations of which five should have been performed independently [Rule 4(c)(i)].

Note: A trained registered medical practitioner (RMP) is permitted to do only first trimester abortions.

Informed Consent

It is essential to obtain an informed consent before an abortion can be done (Rule 8 Form C). The consent form has to be preserved in a sealed cover [Regulation 4(1), MTP Act].

If the woman is 18 years or older, whether married or not, her own written consent is adequate [Section 3(4)(b)MTP Act]. A married woman's husband's consent is not required.

For a woman below 18 years of age or for a mentally unstable woman, the written consent of her guardian is required [Section 3(4)(a), MTP Act].

Legal Position in India

Until 1971 the overwhelming legal position was that except for the *therapeutic abortion,* i.e., terminating a pregnancy to save the life of the mother, causing and procuring abortion was a criminal offence.

Justification for Pre-1971 Statutes

1. To discourage illicit sexual behaviour and promiscuity.
2. To protect a woman from potentially harmful medical procedure.
3. To protect prenatal life.

Fundamental Right to Life and Personal Liberty

Relying on right to privacy emanating from the right to life and personal liberty, the state legalized the right to abortion by enacting Medical Termination of Pregnancy Act.

Person's Right vs. State Interest

The right of a woman to abortion is not an unrestricted right.

The state has right to restrict it emanating from its legitimate interest in

1. protecting the health;
2. protecting the standards of medical practice; and
3. protecting the prenatal life.

Balancing the Interest of the Woman and the Interest of the State

1. Allowing the woman greater freedom of action in the beginning of pregnancy, and
2. the state a greater right to regulate the process as the foetus developed.

Rights Apropos the Duration of Pregnancy

1. The pregnancy is divided into three trimesters of 12 weeks each.
2. In the first trimester, the state has little right to regulate the process; the decision is that of the woman and her physician.
3. During the second trimester, the state's interest increases, at least in the area of protecting the health of the woman.

4. In the third trimester, which begins at 25 weeks' gestation, the state has a predominant interest and right to protect the foetus. A foetus in third trimester is a viable foetus in the sense that it is capable of independent existence.
5. Under the MTP Act in India, a woman's right to seek abortion is restricted to 20 weeks of gestation only. A *non-therapeutic* abortion beyond 20 weeks of gestation is a criminal offence.

The Right to have an Abortion is a Negative Right

The right to abortion is a negative right in the sense that it provides a woman liberty from interference with her body, presuming the conception to be interference with her body. This liberty is like having equal right with all others; to determine what shall or shall not be done to ones body, i.e., a right of self-determination. This right to noninterference does not in itself create a *reciprocal obligation* to provide the means for an abortion.

Non-therapeutic Abortion and Ethics

It is not unethical for a doctor to refuse to undertake a non-therapeutic abortion. It is unethical for a physician to advertise or propagate abortion.

Section 312, Indian Penal Code (IPC)

Under the Indian Penal Code (45 of 1860) inducing abortion or causing "a woman with a child to miscarry" is a criminal offence except when it is done in "good faith to save the life of the woman". Thus, causing an abortion has been legal in India since 1860 when the continuation of pregnancy poses a threat to the life of the mother and if it is considered essential to terminate the pregnancy to save the life of the mother. This was, and still is, a blanket provision for therapeutic abortion without any stipulation as to who can do it, where it can be done or upto what stage of pregnancy it can be done. The only stipulation provided is that it has to be to "save the life of the woman". These missing stipulations are now provided by Section 5 of the Medical Termination of Pregnancy Act.

4

Legal Provisions Related to Criminal Abortions

Criminal Abortions and Professional Ethics

All cases of maternal mortality due to unsafe and unlicensed abortions are cases of double homicide and are required under law (Criminal Procedure Code Section 39 and 174 read with Indian Penal Code Sections 201, 299, 312 and 314) to be reported to the police, subjected to inquest and criminal prosecutions launched. Although a doctor's primary duty is towards her patient and nothing she does should interfere with or delay treatment, it is her public duty, once the patient is under treatment, to report the incident to the authorities at the earliest so that the perpetrator of a criminal abortion is prevented from repeating it. *If she fails in this duty, the doctor is presumed, in the eyes of the law, to be siding with the criminal with a view to shielding him.*

If a doctor submits any case material connected with the criminal abortion for publication in a professional journal, it is presumed that mandatory provision regarding reporting of such a crime to police for investigation has been done. Otherwise the published record may constitute a documented proof of the authors knowledge of such crime which he failed to report as was required by law. The editor of the journal also has a special responsibility here. He must be satisfied that the author(s) reporting the case study have done all that they were legally required to do in that particular case. How they ensure this will depend on the journal's policy and their concern and commitment to prevent criminal abortions. They certainly should not publish a report whose tone suggests concealing the criminal or condoning the crime. A certificate from the authors in the light of ethical clearance certificate insisted for experimental studies and clinical trials may be a pre-requisite to ensure it. A professional medical journal should not publish reports, singly or as compilations, of these cases without such a certificate. If it does so, it would amount to documented defiance of law (having identified the crime, the criminal and the place of its occurrence in the report neither the doctor nor the journal can plead ignorance and innocence). Yet, in what may be construed as defiance of the law, the *Journal of Obstetrics and Gynaecology of India* has been regularly publishing compiled or single accounts of criminal abortions/abortion-deaths as "rare", "unusual", and "interesting" case reports.

There are graphic details of the horrors inflicted by the criminal acts of the illegal abortionists in the individual reports from Muzaffarpur, Murshidabad, Patna, Guwahati, Madras, Thanjavur and Ranchi, published in the *The Journal of Obstetrics and Gynaecology of India* over the past several years, but in none of the reports is there any mention of the steps taken to prevent recurrence of such injuries.

However, illegal abortions are apparently not considered criminal and are not reported to the police as required by the law, even when they prove fatal. The law, further, requires that all unnatural deaths of women within seven years of their marriage should be reported. This attitude is exemplified by the observations of the attending doctors in a case where an illegal abortion done by a 'dai' with the help of stick resulted in deadly gas gangrene sepsis. The case was reported in the *Journal of Obstetrics and Gynaecology of India* and the author, Shakuntala Sahey, states: "As her relatives were not willing, autopsy could not be done". This is despite the fact that that the abortion was done by an unauthorized person and it was a case of unnatural death with manifest evidence of foul play. Exactly the same assertion has been made in a publication: "Autopsy was advised in all these cases, but refused by relatives". In case of death due to criminal abortion or death of a woman within seven years of marriage with evidence that some interference has been done with her body, post-mortem examination is mandatory requirement of police inquest and not a 'choice' of autopsy suggested by the treating doctor/s.

Licensing Death

Does an abortion gain respectability and acceptability if it is done legally in a hospital or clinic? It appears so. Is this matched by a proportionate amount of concern and responsibility on the part of the health personnel when compared to their back-street counterparts? Sadly, no. If the plethora of medical reports is any indication, the liberalization of MTP has brought, in its wake, outright enthusiasm for the procedure, and a disturbing tolerance for various methods in its execution. Such a mindset is typified by the use of *Fetex paste*.

Fetex paste (Gambers Laboratory) was a presumably Ayurvedic preparation though in reality a smorgasbord of chemicals. It was publicized and popularised as an abortifacient paste and widely used by all doctors after it was licensed for this use by the Drugs Controller of India. Thereafter, in case after case, it was reported to cause severe peritonitis, gangrene of internal organs and kidney failure among other complications. In a Thanjavur study covering the years 1964 to 1978, this paste was reported to have been used in 30 per cent of the 747 septic cases that came to the authors' notice. In a typical report from M.G.M. Medical College and M.Y. Hospital, Indore, two of three women died after the use of Fetex paste. The third woman developed renal failure and although she survived, her whole vagina and cervix were sloughed and necrosed. It is a damning reflection on the prevailing professional standards and the efficiency of the drugs control machinery (in India) that, despite reports of severe, adverse, often fatal, effects from the use of this chemical abortifacient paste year after year, nobody asked how this clearly dangerous chemical was permitted to be licensed as an abortifacient at all. Were not the safety trials questioned? Why was use of the paste allowed even after the reports came in of its lethal side effects?

The authors of one report had pleaded: "Advertisements (for Fetex paste) in journals should be stopped and the product should be withdrawn from the market". The *Journal of Obstetrics and Gynaecology of India,* was one such journal advertising Fetex paste. Was it ethical for the *Journal of Obstetrics and Gynecology of India,* the official publication and mouthpiece of the Federation, to have carried this advertisement? Following a spate of these reports in medical journals and the lay press, this presumably Ayurvedic preparation by Gambers Laboratory, was "withdrawn" or was "banned". However, even after its being "withdrawn" or "banned", there followed a report of 34 women who died from septic abortion, a "kutchi" (stick) having been used in 25 women by a "dai"/quack and Fetex paste in three women by general practitioners. Was it ethical for the practitioners of modern medicine to use this Ayurvedic preparation?

Medical Termination of Pregnancy: A Saga of Inhuman Experiments

Any form of physical or chemical interference with the conceptus in the womb is potentially noxious enough to cause abortion, especially in the early stages of pregnancy upto 20 weeks, during which period medical termination of pregnancy (MTP) is legally permitted. Even introduction of a fine needle for aspiration of amniotic fluid for diagnostic purposes not related to MTP may result in abortion. Tragically, this vulnerability of the conceptus simplifies the search for a perfect abortifacient, because all that is left to be ensured is the safety of the pregnant woman! There is a well-known dictum directed to doctors in general and surgeons (including gynaecologists) in particular: "First of all, do no harm". Yet, concern for the pregnant woman was obviously the last thing on the minds of dozens of gynaecologists who launched calculated assaults on their patients in the name of "research". Distilled water, saline in different concentrations, boiling water, various chemicals including corrosives, Fetex paste and rubber catheters, used within or outside the amniotic cavity, alone or in various combinations were experimented and re-experimented with, in thousands of unfortunate women, and the findings reported in the *Journal of Obstetrics and Gynaecology of India* which erred greviously in publishing them. No quality medical journal publishes a report unless the authors satisfy the editors in writing that a competent ethical committee's clearance was obtained and the study was conducted under their supervision. The ethics committee is supposed to give clearance as per the guidelines of the Indian Council of Medical Research. It has to conform to a very strict protocol. Recruitment of patients, especially captive patients, has to be on the basis of informed and free consent. None of the cited "studies" appear to conform to ethical standards for human experiments. How could instillation of distilled water, boiling water, a powdered tablet or rubber catheter be permitted? Imagine the indignity and discomfort from a Foley's catheter (used normally to drain urine from the bladder) introduced into the uterus, its balloon inflated and left in a pregnant lady for 6–18 hours! How does it differ from the use of a sterile stick and cow's urine used by some quacks? And all this was being done to cause non-therapeutic abortion, where the procedure was in no way used to save the life of the mother!

Even if a perverted ethical committee were to give clearance for these macabre trials, there should still have been a major hurdle the "researchers" would need to clear for most of these studies. Very simply, the Drug Controller's permission would have been required. Why? Simply because any substance or device used on the human body is a drug in the eyes of the law, is approved for use only for specific reasons and in a specific formulation; and, when used for different purpose, by a different route, in a different dose schedule or in combination with another agent constitutes a new drug whose human trial needs prior approval of the Drugs Controller of India. It is extremely doubtful if the Drug Controller's permission was sought in these trials. Certainly, since none of the authors stated as much, it may be assumed that no such permission was obtained.

One needs to read these publications in detail to understand the gross indignities inflicted and human right violated. But let me warn you, they make far from pleasant reading. Nupur Lauria and Arpita Bhargav, while medical students at S.M.S. Medical College, Jaipur, compiled data from eleven "research" papers published in 1984 and 1985 in the *Journal of Obstetrics and Gynaecology of India* (*Miscarriage of Medicine: Merciless Assault on Mother's Womb*, Panchsheel Prakashan, Jaipur, 1993). The research groups conducted MTP trials on 2,303 women in the second trimester of pregnancy and respectively used intra-amniotic injection of hypertonic saline in 500 women; distilled water in 250 women; urea with a prostaglandin in 25 women; mid-trimester suction evacuation in 320 women; a combination of prostaglandin by intra-muscular injection with mechanical dilation of the cervix on three groups of 200 women; an array of various methods, namely, hypertonic saline in 200 women, mannitol in nine women, ethacridine lactate in five and a prostaglandin analogue in two rural women; prostaglandin alone and with dilation in 120 women; catheter and prostaglandin in 200 women; vaginal prostaglandin in 62 women; hypertonic saline through the cervix in 120 women as compared with the introduction of a rubber catheter in 120 women; and midtrimester abortion with intra-muscular injection of prostaglandin in 170 women.

There was no logic in repeating these various experiments when the disadvantages of many of them had already been adequately evaluated in earlier trials. There is no evidence that any thought had been given to the planning of these trials to obviate biased inferences. As a result, most of the studies were simply unnecessary, expensive, painful and dangerous exercises. Why, then, were these women subjected to the risks inherent in these studies? Neither clearance from an ethical committee and the Drugs Controller of India nor informed consent from the subjects of these trials was obtained.

This is not to say that there is no room for research in the field of MTP. Given the large number of these procedures being carried out, the field is wide open for serious and beneficial. Take, for example, the cause, nature and treatment of injuries that occur even during MTPs conducted in hospitals, and the lapse that it might have resulted from. A properly done MTP should not cause injury to other structures such as the bladder, rectum or small bowel. If such an injury has occurred, there must be either some unrecognised abnormality in the patient or a procedural lapse must be looked for before labelling it as an inevitable complication that follows any surgical procedure. Such an approach does not attempt to punish the gynaecologist but enables him/her to prevent its occurrence in future.

State-sponsored Birth Control by Abortion: The New Religion of Barbarians

Unsafe abortions, criminal or illegal, in contravention of the provisions of Section 312 of the Indian Penal Code (IPC) and the Medical Termination of Pregnancy (MTP) Act, have thus been a cause of excessive maternal misery, morbidity and mortality, as are human experimentations with various new or novel methods of abortions, undertaken in contravention of the stipulations and guidelines laid down by the Indian Council for Medical Research, the Indian Medical Council and the Drugs Control Authority.

Termination of pregnancy is permitted virtually without question. Medical termination of pregnancy has become a convenient solution to the nuisance of a pregnancy, a pragmatic termination of maternity. Thanks to an ignorant but eager and compliant patient population, especially among the captive poor, who flock the government clinics and hospitals, and a tribe of gynaecologists ever ready to oblige, the Great Indian Abortion Mill never shuts down. Meaty reading for the aficionados of the *Journal of Obstetrics and Gynaecology of India* is assured. Fatal or crippling mishaps go unpublicised. Few complications are challenged.

Criminal Abortions, Unsafe Abortions and Unsafe Experimental Abortions, and the Legal Provisions Regulating Abortions

The Indian Penal Code (IPC) permits a doctor to terminate a pregnancy when, in his considered medical opinion, the continuation of pregnancy poses a "threat to the life" of the mother. Such an abortion is called a therapeutic abortion. The Medical Termination of Pregnancy Act, in addition, permits termination of pregnancy for "grave injury to her physical or mental health". Under Explanation II of sub-section 2 of Section 3 of the MTP Act, contraceptive failure, i.e., "failure of any device or method used by any married woman or her husband for the purpose of limiting the number of children" may be "presumed to constitute grave injury to the mental health of the pregnant woman". Thus, unlike the provisions of IPC 312 that permits therapeutic abortions on the sole discretion of the doctor, sub-section 2, Explanation II of the MTP Act permits a married woman to seek abortion for contraceptive failure. The doctor is exhorted that "in determining whether the continuation of a pregnancy would involve such risk of injury to the health as mentioned in sub-section 2, account may be taken of the pregnant woman's actual or reasonably foreseeable environment" (whatever that means!). The rules and regulations framed under the MTP Act mandate strict stipulations under which pregnancy can be terminated.

Requirements concerning reporting of criminal abortions and interferences that cause death of a woman within seven years of her marriage are mandated in several other provisions of the IPC and Criminal Procedure Code (CrPC). Mandates for human experimentations and drug trials are detailed.

The right to safe abortion has been granted to women as a fundamental right to life and personal liberty under Article 21 of the Constitution of India and codified in the MTP Act, MTP Rules and MTP Regulations. Anybody who inflicts, encourages or condones unsafe abortion in contravention of the codified law, commits a crime. Yet, as we have seen, articles in academic journals describe criminal abortions identifying the person who conducted it, and the place where it was performed. Legally, they are required to report these to the police, at least after treatment is given and certainly if the woman dies. The articles published in the *Journal of Obstetrics and Gynaecology of India* give graphic details of the horrors inflicted by criminal acts of illegal abortionists. None of these mention the steps taken against the culprits to deter repetition of the crime.

So serious is the problem of illegal abortions and the laxity of medical personnel in reporting cases to the law enforcement authorities, that a writ petition was submitted to the Rajasthan Human Rights Commission. The petition is reproduced below:

"The Medical Termination of Pregnancy Act (1971) permits termination of pregnancy upto 20 weeks of gestation for stipulated conditions, in recognized centres, by approved doctors and after stipulated certification by physician/s under strict compliance, monitoring and surveillance of the Medical Termination of Pregnancy Rules (1975) and the Medical Termination of Pregnancy Regulations (1975).

The reported data in the official publication, *Year Book of Family Welfare in India,* reveal that there are over 4 lakh registered abortions done in the country every year of which approximately 40 thousand are in Rajasthan. There is consensus amongst the authorities that in contrast to the number of registered MTPs, illegal abortions in all parts of the country far exceed the reported number, the proportion of legal to illegal abortion being for 1 legal abortion 8 to 9 illegal abortions. Thus, the estimated number of induced abortions in the country every year is 50 to 60 lakhs.

A very high percentage of these illegally done criminal abortions develop severe complications and turn septic and are attended with huge morbidity and mortality.

When a woman develops life threatening complications such as peritonitis, septicaemia, renal failure etc., consequent to induced abortion she lands up in a regular secondary or tertiary care hospital where she is admitted and treated for these complications, and in case of death of the patient, certified to have died due to complication. The fact of criminal interference with her body is not recorded and invariably not reported.

In the recognized format of a death certificate, the underlying (last), antecedent (preceding) and associated causes have all to be mentioned and in that order. For instance, in case of induced abortion leading to perforation of uterus resulting into peritonitis and septicaemia, the order of entry of cause of death in the death certificate would be (a) (underlying) septicemia, (b) (antecedent) peritonitis, and (c) (antecedent) uterine perforation consequent to induced abortion. The cause of death, when extracted from such a certificate, would be induced abortion, the rest of the conditions being complications and sequelae of it.

The doctor who treats the patient for the complication almost never reports the death to the police even though under the law he/she is legally bound to report for inquest by a magistrate. As a result, criminal abortionists are never brought to book and continue their murderous and nefarious activities, killing hundreds of thousand of women in the country.

It is, therefore, prayed that:

1. Chief Medical and Health Officers, Principal Medical and Health Officers and other health care authorities entrusted with the implementation of MTP Act, MTP Rules and MTP Regulations to monitor and ensure safety of medical terminations of pregnancies, especially where it is resorted to for population control measure, should be asked to account for the prevalence of unsafe abortions and for non-detection and prosecution of

criminal abortionists, i.e., abortionists operating outside or in contravention of the MTP Act.

2. The law enforcement authorities be asked to circulate the legal provisions requiring doctors to report all cases of deaths due to induced abortions for inquest by a magistrate.
3. The law enforcement authorities be asked to investigate all cases of death of women within seven years of marriage in which the medical authorities find evidence of some interference with her body.
4. The birth and death registration authorities be asked to send a monthly list of all deaths in women between 18 to 40 years of age along with the certified cause of death to the local health authority for scrutiny".

Criminal Law Provisions Impacting on Criminal Abortions and Foeticide

The Code of Criminal Procedure, 1973

Section 39: Public to give information of certain offences. (1) Every person aware of the commission of, or of the intention of any other person to commit, any offence punishable under any of the following sections of the Indian Penal Code (45 of 1960), namely shall, in the absence of any reasonable excuse, the burden of proving which excuse shall lie upon the person so aware, forthwith give information to the nearest Magistrate or police officer of such commission or intention.

(i) Section 121 to 126 ....

(ii) ....

(iii) ....

(iv) ....

(v) Sections 302, 303 and 304 (that is to say, offences affecting life)

(vi) ....

(xii) ....

(1) For the purpose .... in India.

Section 174: Police to enquire and report on suicide etc. (1) When the officer in charge of a police station or some other police officer specially empowered by the State Government in that behalf receives information that a person has committed suicide, or has been killed by another or by an animal or by machinery or by an accident, or has died under circumstances raising reasonable suspicion that some other person has committed an offence, he shall immediately give intimation thereof to the nearest Executive Magistrate empowered to hold inquest, and, unless otherwise directed by any rule prescribed by the State Government, or by any general or special order of the District or Sub-Divisional Magistrate, shall proceed to the place where the body of such deceased person is, and there, in the presence of two or more respectable inhabitants of the neighbourhood, shall make an investigation, and draw up a report of the apparent cause of death, describing such wounds, fractures, bruises, and other marks of injury as may be found on the body, and stating in what manner, or by what weapon or instrument (if any), such marks appear to be been inflicted.

(2) The report shall be signed by such police officer and other persons, or by so many of them as concur therein, and shall be forthwith forwarded to the District Magistrate or the Sub-Divisional Magistrate.

(3) When

(i) the case involves suicide by a woman within seven years of her marriage, or

(ii) the case relates to the death of a woman within seven years of her marriage in any circumstances raising a reasonable suspicion that some other person committed an offence in relation to such woman, or

(iii) the case relates tom the death of a woman within seven years of her marriage and any relative of the woman has made a request in this behalf or

(iv) there is any doubt regarding the cause of death, or

(v) the police officer for any other reason considers it expedient so to do, he shall, subject to such rules as the State Government may prescribe in this behalf, forward the body, with a view to its being examined, to the nearest Civil Surgeon, or other qualified medical man appointed in this behalf by the State Government, if the state of the weather and the distance admit of its being so forwarded without risk of such putrefaction on the road as would render such examination useless.

(4) The following Magistrates are empowered to hold inquests, namely, any District Magistrate or Sub-Divisional Magistrate and any other Executive Magistrate specially empowered in this behalf by the State Government or the District Magistrate.

The Indian Penal Code, 1860

Section 176: Omission to give notice or information to public servant by person legally bound to give it. Whoever, being legally bound to give any notice or to furnish information on any subject to any public servant, as such, intentionally omits to give such notice or to furnish such information in the manner and at the time required by law, shall be punished with simple imprisonment for a term which may extend to one month, or with fine which may extend to five hundred rupees, or with both

Or, if the notice or information required to be given respects the commission of an offence, or is required for the purpose of preventing the commission of an offence, or in order to the apprehension of an offender, with simple imprisonment for a term which may extend to six months, or with fine which may extend to one thousand rupees, or with both

Or, if the notice or information required to be given is required by an order passed under sub-section (1) of Section 565 of the Code of Criminal Procedure, 1898, with imprisonment of either description for a term which may extend to six months, or with fine which may extend to one thousand rupees, or with both.

Section 201: Causing disappearance of evidence of offence, or giving false information to screen offender. Whoever, knowing or having reason to believe that an offence has been committed, causes any evidence or the commission of that offence to disappear, with intention of screening the offender from legal punishment, or with that intention gives any information respecting the offence which he knows or believes to be false,

If a capital offence, shall if the offence which he knows or believes to have been committed is punishable with death, be punished with imprisonment for either description for a term which may extend to seven years, and shall also be liable to fine,

If punishable with imprisonment for life, and if the offence is punishable with imprisonment for life, or with imprisonment which may extend to ten years, shall be punished with imprisonment of either description for a term which may extend to three years, and shall also be liable to fine,

If punishable with less than ten years' imprisonment, and if the offence is punishable with imprisonment for any term not extending to ten years, shall be punished with imprisonment of the description provided for the offence, for a term which may extend to one-fourth part of the longest term of the imprisonment provided for the offence, or with fine, or with both.

Section 202: Intentional omission to give information of offence by person bound to inform. Whoever, knowing or having reason to believe that an offence has been committed, intentionally omits to give any information respecting that offence which he is legally bound to give, shall be punished with imprisonment of either description for a term which may extend to six months, or with fine, or with both.

Section 299: Culpable homicide. Whoever causes death by doing an act with the intention of causing death, or with the intention of causing such bodily injury as is likely to cause death, or with the knowledge that he is likely by such act to cause death, commits the offence of culpable homicide.

Explanation 3: The causing of the death of a child in the mother's womb is not homicide. But it may amount to culpable homicide to cause the death of living child, if any part of the that child has been brought forth, though the child may not have breathed or been completely born.

Section 300: Murder. Except in the cases hereinafter excepted, culpable homicide is murder, if the act by which the death is caused is done with the intention of causing death, or

secondly, if it is done with the intention of causing such bodily injury as the offender knows to be likely to cause the death of the person to whom the harm is caused, or

thirdly, if it is done with he intention causing bodily injury to any person and the bodily injury intended to be inflicted is sufficient in the ordinary course of nature to cause death, or

fourthly, if the person committing the act knows that it is so imminently dangerous that it must, in all probability, cause death or such bodily injury as is likely to cause death, and commits such act without any excuse for incurring the risk of causing death or such injury as aforesaid.

Exception 1. When culpable homicide is not murder. Culpable homicide is not murder if the offender, whilst deprived of the power of self-control by grave and sudden provocation, causes the death of the person who gave the provocation or causes the death of any person by mistake or accident.

The above exception is subject to the following provisos:

First: That the provocation is not sought or voluntarily provoked by the offender as an excuse for killing or doing harm to any person.

Secondly: That provocation is not given by anything done in obedience to the law, or by public servant in the lawful exercise of the powers of such public servant.

Thirdly: That the provocation is not given by anything done in the lawful exercise of the right of private defence.

Exception 2. Culpable homicide is not murder if the offender, in the exercise of good faith of the right of private defence or person or property exceeds the power given to him by law and causes the death or the person against whom he is exercising such right of defence without premeditation, and without, and without any intention of doing more harm than is necessary for the purpose of such defence.

Exception 3. Culpable homicide is not murder if the offender, being a public servant or aiding a public servant acting for the advancement of public justice, exceeds the powers given to him by law, and causes death by doing an act which he, in good faith, believes to be lawful and necessary for the due discharge of his duty as such public servant and without ill-will towards the person whose death is caused.

Exception 4. Culpable homicide is not murder if it is committed without premeditation in sudden fight in the heat of passion upon sudden quarrel and without the offender's having taken undue advantage or acted in a cruel or unusual manner.

Exception 5. Culpable homicide is not murder when the person whose death is caused, being above the age of eighteen years, suffers death or takes the risk of death with his own consent.

Section 301: Culpable homicide by causing death of person other than person whose death was intended. If a person, by doing anything which he intends or knows to be likely to cause death, commits culpable homicide by causing the death of any person, whose death he neither intends nor knows himself to be likely to cause, the culpable homicide committed by the offender is of the description of which it would have been if he had caused the death of the person whose death he intended or knew himself to be likely to cause.

Section 302: Punishment for murder. Whoever commits murder shall be punished with death, or imprisonment for life, and shall also be liable to fine.

Section 304: Punishment for culpable homicide not amounting to murder. Whoever commits culpable homicide not amounting to murder, shall be punished with imprisonment for life, or imprisonment of either description for a term which may extend to ten years, and shall also be liable to fine, if the act by which the death is caused is done with the intention of causing death, or of causing such bodily injury as is likely to cause death,

Or, with imprisonment of either description for a term which may extend to ten years, or with fine, or with both, if the act is done with the knowledge that it is likely to cause death, but without any intention to cause death or to cause such bodily injury as is likely to cause death.

Section 304A: Causing death by negligence. Whoever causes the death of any person by doing any rash or negligent act not amounting to culpable homicide shall be punished with imprisonment of either description for a term which may extend to two years, or with fine, or with both.

Section 307: Attempt to murder. Whoever does any act with such intention or knowledge, and under such circumstances that, if that act caused death, he would be guilty of murder, shall be punished with imprisonment of either description for a term which may extend to ten years, and shall also be liable to fine; and, if hurt is caused to any person by such act, the offender shall be liable either to imprisonment for life, or to such punishment as is hereinbefore mentioned.

Section 308: Attempt to commit culpable homicide. Whoever does any act with such intention or knowledge and under such circumstances that, if he by that act caused death, he would be guilty of culpable homicide not amounting to murder, shall be punished with imprisonment of either description for a term which may extend to three years, or with fine, or with both; and, if hurt is caused to any person by such act, shall be punished with imprisonment of either description for a term which may extend to seven years, or with fine, or with both.

Section 312: Causing miscarriage. Whoever voluntarily causes a woman with child to miscarry shall, if such miscarriage be not caused in good faith for the purpose of saving the life of the woman, be punished with imprisonment of either description for a term which may extend to three years, or with fine, or with both; and if the woman be quick with child, shall be punished with imprisonment of either description for a term which may extend to seven years, and shall also be liable to fine.

Explanation: A woman who causes herself to miscarry, is within the meaning of this section.

Section 313: Causing miscarriage without woman's consent. Whoever commits the offence defined in the last preceding section without the consent of woman, whether the woman is quick with child or not, shall be punished with imprisonment of life, or with imprisonment of either description for a term which may extend to ten years, and shall also be liable to fine.

Section 314: Death caused by act done with intent to cause miscarriage. Whoever, with intent to cause the miscarriage of a woman with child, does any act which causes the death of such woman, shall be punished with imprisonment of either description for a term which may extend to ten years, and shall also be liable to fine.

If act done without woman's consent – and if the act is done without the consent of the woman, shall be punished either with imprisonment for life, or with punishment above mentioned.

Explanation: It is not essential to this offence that the offender should know that the act is likely to cause death.

Section 315: Act done with intent to prevent child being born alive or to cause it to die after birth. Whoever before the birth of any child does any act with the intention of thereby preventing that child from being born alive or causing it to die after its birth, and does by such act prevent that child from being born alive, or causes it to die after its birth, shall, if such act be not caused in good faith for the purpose of saving the life of the mother be punished with imprisonment of either description of a term which may extend to ten years, or with fine, or with both.

Section 316: Causing death of quick unborn child by act amounting to culpable homicide. Whoever does any act under such circumstances, that if he thereby caused death he would be guilty of culpable homicide, and does by such act cause the death of a quick unborn child, shall be punished with imprisonment of either description for a term which may extend to ten years, and shall also be liable to fine.

Further Readings

Bhatt, S. and S. Bandi. 'The Dangerous Fetex Paste', *J. Obst. & Gyn. of India,* 1985, Vol. 35: 27–29.

Biswas, C., N. Bhattacharya, A.K. Maity, B.K. Goswami and Mukherji. 'Bowel Injury: A Menace in the Era of Liberalisation of Abortion', *J. of Obst. & Gyn. of India,* 1997, Vol. 47: 419–424.

Desai, Pankaj and Purvi Patel. 'Prospective Comparative Evaluation of Intra-amniotic versus Extra-amniotic Routes for Ethacridine Lactate for Second Trimester MTP: No Difference', *J. of Obst. & Gyn. of India,* 2001, Vol. 51(6): 158–160.

Jayaram, V. Kamla and G. Ratna. 'Mid-trimester Termination of Pregnancy with Extra Amniotic PGF 2 ALFA and Comparative Study with Normal Saline and Iodine Saline', *J. of Obst. & Gyn. of India,* 1996, Vol. 46: 614–617.

Kaur, Devinder, Sukhvider Shergill, A.S. Saini and Navdeep Singh. 'Comparative Evaluation of Ethacridine Lactate, Normal Saline and Distilled Water in Mid-trimester Abortions', *J. of Obst. & Gyn. of India,* 1997; Vol. 47: 160–163.

Kini M., Pravin and N. Rajgopal. 'Medically Induced (Non-Surgical) Early First Trimester Abortion With Mifepristone (RU 486) and Multidose Misoprostol', *J. of Obst. & Gyn. of India,* 1996, Vol. 46: 470–476.

Nayak, Arun H., Bhavana P. Shah and Chandni M. Alwani. 'Extra-amniotic Instillation of Tablet Primprost with Ethacridine Lactate for Termination of Second Trimester Pregnancy', *J. of Obst. & Gyn. of India,* 1996, Vol. 46:753–758.

Patel, Babu S., Nimish C. Pandya, Manish M. Jadav, Malvika K. Bhatt, B.S. Ankleshwaria. 'Deaths Attibutable to Tubal

Sterilization – 1979 to 1999', *J. of Obst. & Gyn. of India,* 2001; Vol. 51(2): 127.

Rani, P. Reddi, A. Bupathy and S. Balsubramanian. 'Maternal Mortality Due to Septic Abortion'. *J. of Obst. & Gyn of India,* 1996, Vol. 46: 73–76.

Rao, A. Arun. 'Ischiorectal Abscess: Sequalae to Criminal Abortion', *J. of Obst. & Gyn. of India,* 1996, Vol. 46: 165–166.

Sharma, J.B., U. Manaktala, Ashok Kumar and M. Malhotra. Complications and Management of Septic Abortions: A Five Year Study', *J. of Obst. & Gyn. of India,* 2001, Vol. 51(6): 74–76.

Singh, Anita, Himanshu Roy, Punam Dixit, Neelam Manav, Shipra Roy and Shanti Roy. 'Termination of Pregnancy' by Combined Intrauterine Catheter and Laminaria Tent, *J. of Obst. & Gyn. of India,* 1996, Vol. 46: 618–623.

Sinha, Renuka and Manju M. Bara. 'Maternal Mortality in Unsafe Abortion', *J. of Obst. & Gyn. of India,* 2001, Vol. 51(2): 123–125.

5

Medicine Deranged

Indian Statism and Nazism: A Saga of Human Rights Violations in Reproductive Health

State-sponsored/blessed medicine in India closely parallels the Nazi medical practice. The insidious co-opting of the medical profession by the state to implement its socio-economic policies through medical solutions, the silent acquiescence of the medical profession in inflicting compromised and barbarous medicare on the population in the name of socialism and welfare, with over 5,000 unnecessary deaths every year due to septic abortions and ill-performed sterilization interventions alone, and the totality of the medical violence since independence, would shame even the Nazis.

Thanks to the pressure of the international community (read developed nations), India today has been converted into a concentration camp for women of reproductive age. To live their reproductive lives they are at the mercy of the state and the state-co-opted NGOs. For the great cause of population control, promoted and financed by international agencies, no means are improper, no holds are barred. Ethical considerations are considered senseless niceties for the fast multiplying natives. Safety norms, for the same reason and for reasons of urgency, are impractical and unpragmatic. Preventive depopulation by contraception and promotive depopulation by medical termination of pregnancy (the births 'averted' and the births 'prevented' of population controllers) are the state enforced medical solutions to the social problem of poverty. Infanticides for reasons of poverty, though sporadic and few, were considered barbarous, and justly so. But, the elimination of five million foetuses through MTPs for the same reason of poverty brings international acclaim and huge funds (the reward). Deaths of thousands of women in the process, due to septic abortions and improperly performed tubectomies, are overlooked with impunity. The overtly barbarous individual-perpetrated occasional infanticide has been replaced with state-organized mass elimination of foetuses and females. The overt cruelty of individuals has been replaced with the covert Nazism of the state. This is preventive elimination of the poor as a part of the poverty control programme.

De-population is a Nazi concept of development. While Hitler practised it in Germany, developed countries are practising it in India. Liability to become pregnant is the deadliest illness – eugenic preventive medicine is geared to eradicate it as far as possible. For women in the reproductive age group, India is a large concentration camp where neo-Nazis operating as population experts, eliminate foetuses and females in the name of welfare.

Non-therapeutic abortions (abortions other than those performed to save the live of the mother) are freely promoted, aggressively marketed and effectively enforced by the state-co-opted medical professionals. The unabashed enthusiasm to undertake non-therapeutic interventions is unethical, to say the least. But then, ethics are the first casualty when the state drafts medical men to counter social pathologies and to solve social problems.

Contraception is not a choice; it is a state demand. Medical termination of pregnancy is not a reproductive the right of women for unwanted pregnancies (to be exercised in the first 12 weeks), but an aggressively pursued state policy of de-population (upto 20 weeks by law and thereafter by default).

Laparoscopy Deaths

State-blessed depopulation programmes that can go terribly wrong are best exemplified by sterilization drives. Consider in this regard the following account of four sudden deaths in laparoscopic sterilization camps in North Bengal published in official organ of the Federation of Obstetrics and Gynaecology of India – *The Journal of Obstetrics and Gynaecology of India.** The relevant details from the paper are extracted below: "Number of cases attending each camp varied from 25 to 500 cases per day per two surgeons. Therefore, thorough clinical screening of all the patients before operation could not be done."

Ethical Questions

1. Is it ethical for medical professionals to agree to undertake more cases (elective cases) than can be handled under basic scientific norms?
2. Is it ethical to operate on a patient without 'thorough' clinical examination?

"One case expired following sedation only. Half-an-hour after sedation (Inj. Pethidine-100 mg, Phenargan 25–50 mg and Inj. Atropine I.M.) she was put to O.T. (operation table?) where uterus was found to be 24 weeks size due to pregnancy, which she concealed; she was sent back to pre-operative room where she fell asleep. During sleep she expired which was detected after four hours, the exact time of death was unnoticed."

According to the authors, "In the first case, who was moderately anaemic, pethidine and phenargan might have produced hypotension and respiratory depression (Parikh, 1985) which was unnoticed until her death. Moreover, she was starving for almost 24 hours causing hypoglycaemia resulting in less uptake of oxygen by the vital centres of medulla (respiratory, cardiac and vasomotor) which became

* Sarkar, B. and Bhadra, R.N. (1989) Sudden Deaths during Laparoscopic Sterilisation in Camps, *Journal of Obstetrics and Gynaecology of India,* Vol. 39, pp. 231–235.

subnormal in their function. Brain-stem reticular formation also became less active resulting in a stuporous condition which probably became worse by the depressive action of the sedative applied on the reticular activating system (RAS)."

Ethics

1. Is failure to recognize 24 weeks pregnancy during preoperative medical screening an acceptable oversight?
2. Is it acceptable from doctors who are aware that injection of pethidine and phenargan may cause hypotension and respiratory depression, if they leave the patient unmonitored and unattended, especially if the patient has been kept starving for 24 hours and is likely to become hypoglycaemic?
3. Can death from pre-anaesthetic medication be certified a natural death without an investigation.

The doctor-authors provide the following details of the other three cases that died: "Other three cases expired within 2–3 minutes following the completion of pneumo-peritonium. Series of events were like this: subumbilical infiltration of 1 per cent lignocaine was given in one case and no local anaesthesia was given in other two cases. Pneumo-peritonium was done without any difficulty by about two litters (*sic*) of oxygen at a rate of one litter per minute."

Ethical Questions

1. Was it proper to do the procedure without local anaesthesia in the two cases? Why was it not required or necessary in the two cases?
2. Is it ethical and legal to use oxygen in place the mandatory carbon di-oxide?

"Immediately after the withdrawal of the Veress needle whole body of the patient went into convulsive movements with rigidity for a short while; they became unconscious; veins of the lower extremities unto the hips were engorged. Respiration, heart sounds and peripheral pulse were gradually slowing down in both rate and volume and ultimately stopped within 2–3 minutes."

Ethics

1. Was it ethical for the doctors to just watch the patients – not one but three – convulse to death from what they thought was the pneumoperitoneum they had done with two litres of oxygen?

"In present series oxygen was used as the insufflating agent in all the cases, which was used directly from the oxygen cylinder to the Veress needle through polythene tubing. Oxygen was used because of its easier availability than CO2 or N2O. But as the oxygen cylinder cannot be used in the carbon di-oxide pneumo apparatus because of absence of fitting arrangement, increased intraperitoneal pressure could not be read."

Ethics

1. Is it ethical and legal for supervisory authorities to permit laparoscopic tubectomy without ensuring mandatory surgical norms of use of carbon di-oxide under monitored pressure with pneumo apparatus and thereby risk the life of women undergoing the operation?
2. Is it ethical for doctors to agree to work under compromised surgical norms?
3. No autopsy was done. The three deaths, the doctors conjecture, occurred due to the effect of intra-abdominal pressure on inferior venacava, pushing up of diaphragm and noxious nerve reflexes. An equally plausible possibility is that the blindly introduced Veress needle entered a vein (a well-recognized possibility) through which two litre of oxygen, a gas sparsely soluble in blood, was pushed with uncontrolled pressure. The insoluble oxygen must have formed an embolus of a ball of bubbles (the doctors discount the possibility because, as they state, mill-machine murmur was not heard) that blocked the vessel taking the blood to the lungs - what the doctors call massive pulmonary embolism.

   In either case were these simple laparoscopic deaths?
4. Who should be held responsible for these deaths - the doctors?, the supervisors of the camps?, or the state at

whose behest these non-therapeutic interventions were done under compromised conditions?

5. Do not the editors and publisher of the journal have an ethical liability for publishing such a report as a research paper?

This was in a 1989 publication. More than a decade later, it seems that the attitude of the professionals has not changed. In 2001, in a report of deaths following laparoscopic sterilization, the authors report 16 deaths, summarizing that "deaths due to family welfare programme is (*sic*) tragic, painful and unbearable as it is always premature and preventable".*

Yet, in the paper, the cause of death, i.e., the injury that proved fatal, the circumstances in which it occurred and the deficiency or lapse in the individual case has not been elucidated or even alluded to, to make the reader wiser to avoid similar lapse.

For prevention of such injuries they make a platitudinal general statement (obviously from book text): "Use of endotracheal intubation for general anaesthesia, particularly for laparoscopic sterilization, careful insertion of needle and trochar, strict follow up of standard infection control measure in and outside operation theatres, prophylactic use of broad spectrum antibiotics and discontinuation of oral contraceptive prior to sterilization may help to prevent sterilization attributable deaths."

The basis of such recommendation and conclusions is missing. Is it to be presumed that in the aforesaid cases these norms were not followed and hence the fatal injuries? The authors must elucidate the possible constraints or mitigating circumstances because of which in each case the required norms could not be followed. As in the absence of the same it would amount to gross negligence and homicide by rash or negligent act. The editors have permitted them to gloss over the essential issue.

---

* Deaths Attributable to Tubal Sterilization - 1979 to 1999 by Babu S. Patel, Nimish C. Pandya, Manish M. Jadav, Malvika K. Bhatt and B.S. Ankleshwaria, J. *Obst. & Gyn. of India,* 2001, Vol. 51, pp. 126–129.

The appropriateness of the treatment of injury and the final event that caused death are based on biased interpretations, presumptions and conjectures and are not based on independent investigation. This is not how hospital deaths are investigated – deaths of healthy women in whom non-therapeutic interference has been done. No one would be wiser by reading these reports.

Finally, the statement of the authors: "Autopsy was advised in all these cases, (pulmonary embolism) but refused by relatives."

Autopsy in these cases (death of married women within seven years of marriage) is part of mandatory inquest by a magistrate.

This report is not as crude as the 1989 report but certainly not an ethical presentation fit for publication in official organ of professional association.

Now look at the state-sponsored depopulation by abortions.

Unsafe abortions, criminal or illegal, in contraventions of the provisions of Section 312 IPC and MTP Act, have been a cause of excessive maternal morbidity, mortality and misery. Acceptable safe methods appropriate for termination of pregnancy in 1st and 2nd trimesters are detailed and constitute the present-day norms for termination of pregnancy. Human experimentations with various new or novel methods of abortions, undertaken in contraventions of stipulations and guidelines laid down by the Indian Council of Medical Research (ICMR), the Indian Medical Council (IMC) and Drugs Control Authority, fall in the same category.

6

Abortion Pills: Murder Marketed

Here are reproduced two letters addressed to the Drugs Controller of Rajasthan and the Chairman, Rajasthan Human Rights Commission, respectively, regarding the mal-distribution and marketing of abortion pills in Rajasthan. This will be followed by the presentation of the rejoinder on MTP pills to Rajasthan Human Rights Commission and its decision in a case delivered on March 20, 2004.

The Drugs Controller of Rajasthan, Directorate of Health Services, Jaipur

I draw your kind attention to the distribution and marketing of the MIFEPRISTONE and MISOPROSTOL abortion pills by the Sun, Cipla and Zydus Alidac Pharmaceuticals in Jaipur. I have gathered from the practicing gynaecologists that it is being supplied to the practicing gynecologists to be given to the willing patients after obtaining consent from the patient. The money is to be collected from the patient by the physician, which in turn is to be "collected" by the drug representative. This is highly irregular, unethical and illegal and cannot be equated with drug dispensing by primary physicians at their dispensary.

Besides the drug is meant for medical termination of pregnancy (MTP). As per the provisions of the MTP Act 1971, termination of pregnancy under the Act can be done only by an APPROVED PHYSICIAN, IN AN APPROVED CENTRE AND FOR APPROVED CONDITIONS ONLY (threat to mother's life, congenital anomalies, rape induced pregnancy and pregnancy due to contraceptive failure, the last only in case of married women).

The pill as per the promotional literature is to be distributed for abortion at home. This is contrary to the provisions of MTP Act. It makes no difference that as per the consent form circulated by the drug companies and to be signed by the patient, states that the patient agrees to take the pill in the physician's clinic. As per the MTP Act, a gynecologist's consulting chamber is not recognized for induced abortion (MTP). In any case, the abortion takes place at home and is not in conformity with the MTP Act. The possibility of failure and profuse bleeding are substantial and would expose the patient to grave, even fatal risk, especially in rural settings. The risk is still greater in unwed teen-age girls who may abort and bleed at home. This is virtually marketing murder for paltry monetary gains.

Also the distribution of full text articles reproduced from *New England Journal of Medicine, British Journal of Obstetrics and Gynaecology, Journal of American Medical Women's Association,* as a drug-promotion material, with or without the permission of the journals and the authors, is unethical. It amounts to lending the name by authors for promotion of brand/drug and amounts "ASSOCIATION" under the MCI Act.

Kindly investigate the matter and take such measures as are available under law to prevent this unsafe promotion and distribution of abortion pills to the patients.

***

The Chairman, Human Rights Commission, Rajasthan, Jaipur

I draw your kind attention to the distribution and marketing of Mifepristone and Misoprostol tablets manufactured by Sun, Cipla and Zydus Alidac Pharmaceuticals. These tablets for abortion are supplied to practicing gynecologists to be given to patients after obtaining their consent. The money is to be collected from the patient by the physician, who in turn turns it over to the drug representative. This is highly irregular, unethical and illegal and cannot be equated with drug dispensing by primary physicians at their dispensary.

Second, the drug is meant for medical termination of pregnancy (MTP). This must be done, according to the MTP Act, 1971, only by an approved physician, in an approved centre and for approved conditions (threat to mother's life, congenital anomalies, rape-induced pregnancy and pregnancy due to contraceptive failure, the last only in the case of married women).

According to the promotional literature of the pharmaceuticals, the pills are to be distributed for abortion at home. This is contrary to the provisions of the MTP Act, which specifically stipulates that MTP can be done only in an approved centre. An abortion induced in contravention of the MTP Act is punishable under Section 312 and related sections of the Indian Penal Code. The pharmaceutical companies are trying to circumvent this by supplying a consent form that is to be got signed from the MTP seeking woman by the gynecologist in her consulting chamber. It makes no difference that in the consent form circulated by the drug companies and to be signed by the patient, the patient agrees to take the pill in the physician's clinic. According to the MTP Act, a gynecologist's consulting chamber is not recognized for the purpose of induction of MTP. In any case, an abortion induced in a gynecologist's consulting chamber, in fact' will occur at the woman's home which is not in conformity with the MTP Act, as the life threatening complications occur at the time of final abortion. The possibility of failure and profuse bleeding is substantial and is likely to occur in about 5 per cent of cases as per the literature supplied by the pharmaceuticals. This would expose the patients to grave risks, especially in rural settings. The risk is greater for unwed women for whom pregnancy is looked down upon, and who may, therefore, not contact proper services and may abort and bleed at home. It is specifically to take care of these anticipated and known life-threatening hazards and complications that the MTP Act mandates that MTPs should be done in only approved centres where facilities to deal with these anticipated life threatening complications are available. The pharmaceutical companies are trying to circumvent this safety provision by asking the gynecologist to include in the consent form a clause that the MTP seeking woman has been intimated about the availability of such facilities.

Besides, the pill is being distributed through qualified and unqualified medical practitioners in the country, though under the MTP Act only a practitioner registered under The Indian Medical Council Act can terminate a pregnancy.

Now, the pills have been made available at the drug stores. Even though they can be supplied only on prescription of a registered medical practitioner, in the prevalent conditions in the country they will be freely available over the drug stores counter.

This is virtually marketing murder by the pharmaceuticals for monetary gains with the open connivance of medical professionals and the drugs control authority.

Also, the distribution of full-text articles reproduced from the *New England Journal of Medicine, British Journal of Obstetrics and Gynecology* and the *Journal of American Medical Women's Association* as promotional material, with or without the permission of the journals and the authors, is unethical. It amounts to lending the name by authors for promotion of a brand/drug and amounts to 'association' under the MCI Act.

This marketing strategy to promote the abortion pill as an unsupervised at home MTP (abortion) method is dangerous and will claim hundreds of lives from the expected known sequelae and complications of induced abortion (MTP). In the prevalent health care scenario in India with very lax and almost non-existent regulatory mechanism, unsafe abortion under the garb of MTP is already claiming hundreds of lives in the country.

I enclose here with the letter that I had addressed to the Drugs Controller of Rajasthan who is the statutory regulatory authority to take action in the matter. The reply received from them is also enclosed, which shows that nothing in the matter has been done except to forward copies of the letter to other functionaries. The matter is too grave and urgent to be left to such routine handling.

I earnestly request the Commission to issue notices to

1. The Drugs Controller of Rajasthan, Directorate of Health Service, Jaipur.
2. The Drugs Controller of India, through the Drugs Controller of Rajasthan.
3. Sun, Cipla and Zydus Alidac pharmaceutical companies, through the Drugs Controller of Rajasthan, Jaipur.
4. Director of Health Services, Rajasthan, Directorate of Health Services, Jaipur.
5. Rajasthan Medical Council and through them the Medical Council of India, New Delhi.

They may place before the Commission all relevant details about licensing, marketing, promotion and distribution of the abortion pills, to answer to the aforesaid unsafe distribution of the abortion pills. Appropriate action may then be taken against the perpetrators of human rights violations.

I shall be grateful to be given an opportunity to personally appear before the Commission to submit the details.

***

Rejoinder on MTP Pills to Rajasthan Human Rights Commission

Progesterone is a hormone secreted by the body that retains and sustains pregnancy. Mifepristone or RU486 is a drug that antagonizes the effect of progesterone secreted by the body. When administered to a pregnant woman, it stops the growth of pregnancy. The foetus, therefore, dies in the uterus. Misoprostol simulates the effect of prostaglandin, which causes contraction of the uterus. When administered after Mifepristone, the uterus undergoes powerful contraction and expels the already dead foetus.

Mifepristone has been approved for abortion (termination of pregnancy). This drug is approved under Drugs & Cosmetics Act exclusively for use as an abortifacient only. Misoprostol, in contrast, is approved as a prostaglandin analogue for several uses, especially as an anti-ulcer drug. It is contra-indicated in normal pregnancy. At the end of pregnancy, it is given to cause contraction of uterus to expel its contents.

Zydus, Sun Pharma and Cipla are marketing Mifepristone to terminate the pregnancy and Misoprostol to expel the dead foetus. The two drugs together are marketed under their proprietary names by the three pharmaceutical companies to be administered to cause medical termination of pregnancy (MTP) of less than 49 days duration. They are not marketed as a combination drug but as a package of two drugs to be taken one after the other at an interval of two days.

The Drugs Controller of India has approved Mifepristone as an abortifacient to be manufactured, marketed and sold with mandatory stipulations under the various provisions of the Drugs and Cosmetics Act. Mifepristone is approved to be made available for Medical Termination of Pregnancy (MTP) strictly under the provisions of Medical Termination of Pregnancy Act, 1971 (MTP Act). Under the MTP Act, pregnancy can be terminated by (1) approved physicians, (2) in approved centres, (3) for approved indications, and (4) for approved duration. The MTP Rules and MTP Regulations govern each of these four stipulations.

As per the aforesaid legal provisions, the doctors approved under the MTP Act can do MTP. All qualified physicians registered under MCI Act cannot do it. Only those who meet the stipulated approval criteria under the MTP Act can do it. It is only these approved doctors who can, under the law, prescribe and administer Mifepristone. Also under the MTP Act, termination of pregnancy can be done in approved centres. The list of centres approved for MTP by Director of Health Services is available with the Directorate of Health Services.

Mifepristone is approved by the Drugs Controller of India to be prescribed and administered by doctors approved under the MTP Act to terminate pregnancy at centres approved under the MTP Act. The pharmaceutical companies are to market the drug in conformity with the MTP Act for which it has been specifically approved.

The pharmaceutical companies, however, are making it available at all drug stores. The drug stores are dispensing it on the prescription of any registered practitioner, in contravention of the of the stipulation that it can be sold for administration by a physician approved under the MTP Act and attached to and practicing MTP at an approved MTP centre.

The pharmaceutical companies, as per their promotional literature distributed to doctors, are openly flouting the provisions of law by circumventing the stipulations and making it freely available to all doctors to induce termination of pregnancy at home.

Mifepristone-Misoprostol drug regime causes successful termination of pregnancy in 92–94 per cent of cases. In a percentage of failed cases, it causes severe bleeding which may prove fatal unless immediate surgical evacuation of the uterus is undertaken with or without blood transfusion support.

It is, therefore, mandatory that a standby operation theatre and blood transfusion facility too should be available where medical termination of pregnancy is done by Mifepristone-Mesoprostol method. In the absence of this a large number of women will bleed to death at home. Presently 40 50 lakh abortions (MTPs) are done in the country of which 70to 80 percent are early below 12 weeks abortions. This frightening scenario with free, and frequently over-the-counter, sale of Mifepristone, especially in towns and villages where recognized MTP centres are not available. Neither are operative surgical facilities and blood transfusion facilities available for those who are expected to bleed severely consequent to unsuccessful administration of abortion drug regime.

Those who make available Mifepristone to be administered in contravention of the provisions of the Drugs & Cosmetics Act and the MTP Act along with those who prescribe and administer it in contravention of the Acts are liable to be prosecuted under provisions of the Indian Penal Code in addition to the provisions of the two Acts.

The State Drugs Controller responsible for implementation of the Drugs & Cosmetics Act and the Director of Health Services who is responsible for implementation of MTP Act, are individually and jointly responsible and competent to take action against the defaulters.

Physicians are as much liable for the contravention of the Drugs & Cosmetics Act as are the pharmaceutical companies for their acts of commission and omission under the MTP Act.

The Human Rights Commission may therefore kindly issue directions that:

1. Free sale of Mifepristone preparations from drug stores on prescription of any registered medical practitioner be stopped as it is contrary to the mandatory stipulations imposed by the Drugs Controller of India.
2. Unauthorized general physicians be directed not to prescribe Mifepristone as the same would constitute violation of the legal provisions.
3. State Drugs Controller be directed to ensure that Mifepristone is dispensed only on the prescription of doctors approved for MTP who are attached to centres approved for MTP by the Director of Health services and, if possible, to ensure that the drug Mifepristone be supplied only to the approved MTP centres.

***

Decision of Rajasthan Human Rights Commission in Case No. 03/17/260, delivered on March 20, 2004

Before dealing with the main questions involved in these two petitions, we may say a few words by way of prelude by reproducing a passage from an article:

"Addressing Sex Selection and the Right to Abortion" by Asmita Basu, Project Coordinator (Health) with the 'Women's Rights Initiative Unit of the Lawyer's Collective', New Delhi.

"Recent news reports and the 2001 Census data indicate a grim demographic picture of declining female to male ratios. Other than population imbalances, this brings in its wake, associated social problems of increased violence against women, sexual abuse, trafficking, forced polyandry .... the list is endless.

The most obvious reason behind this alarming decline is the proliferation of diagnostic technologies that are easily and cheaply available, the most popular method is this regard being ultra-sonography. The popularity of this technique is also based on the fact that it is non-invasive and has no documented adverse side effects.

Implementation of laws curbing sex determinative tests is met with huge impediments as this technique is also widely used for routine diagnostic tests on most pregnant women. Given the fact that records under the Pre-Natal Diagnostic (Regulation and Prevention of Misuse) Techniques Act, 1996 (PNDTA) are rarely maintained, it is almost impossible to regulate persons carrying out these tests. Hence, it is essential to look at other avenues to cub the incidence of sex selective abortions".

Sex determination tests ultimately end in the termination of pregnancy and, therefore, we would consider the matter in the light of abortion laws.

Abortion or causing of miscarriage is an offence punishable under sections 312-316 of the Indian Penal Code. However, if the miscarriage was caused under good faith of the purpose of saving the life of the women, it would not be an offence. In spite of all these penal provisions, a large number of illegal and unsafe abortions take place and, therefore, a concern for this practice was raised sometime in the mid-60s. It was thereafter that Medical Termination of Pregnancy Act, 1971 was passed by the Parliament. It came into force on April 1, 1072. Under this Act, Medical Termination of Pregnancy (for short, MTP) can be done only by the medical practitioners registered under this Act and that too at a government hospital or centre recognized by the government for that purpose particularly where the stipulated surgical facilities and facilities for blood transfusion are available. It may be stated that under the MTP Act, MTP can be done where a pregnant woman has a serious medical disease and continuation of pregnancy would endanger her life. While in the pregnancy upto 12 weeks, opinion of one doctor is enough but where the pregnancy exceeds 12 weeks but is below 20 weeks, opinion and approval of two registered medical practitioners is necessary.

Now, abortion can be induced by different methods depending on the weeks of pregnancy completed. In the instant case, however, we are concerned only with the medical methods in the first trimester. The main drug to which an objection has been taken by Dr. S.G. Kabra (petitioner) is that "Mifepristone", also known as RU-486, which is used for bringing about MTP is being freely sold across the counter and is, therefore, being misused and abused resulting sometimes in the death of the pregnant woman on account of excessive bleeding. It is contended by him that this drug can be sold only on the prescription of a registered gynaecologist for use either in the hospital or at the recognized centres where necessary facilities for bringing about the termination of pregnancy are available including the facility for blood transfusion. The complaint of Dr. Kabra is that on account of free sale of the drug across the counter, anybody can purchase it and give it to the pregnant woman especially in the rural areas where may women have been found to die on account of excessive bleeding or other complications. Dr. Kabra has also stated in this petition as under:

"The Medical Termination of Pregnancy Act (1971) permits termination of pregnancy upto 20 weeks of gestation for stipulated conditions, of approved centres, by approved doctors and after stipulated certification by physician/s under strict compliance, monitoring and surveillance of the Medical Termination of Pregnancy Rules (1975) and the Medical Termination of Pregnancy Regulations (1975).

The reported data in the official publication, *Year Book of Family Welfare in India*, reveal that there are over 4 lakh registered abortions done in the country every year of which approximately 40 thousand are in Rajasthan.

There is consensus amongst the authorities that in contrast to the number of registered MTPs, illegal abortions in all parts the country far exceed the reported number, the proportion of legal to illegal abortion being for 1 legal abortion 8 to 9 illegal abortions. Thus, the estimated number of induced abortions in the country every year is 50 to 60 lakh.

A very high percentage of these illegally done criminal abortions develop severe complications and turn septic and are attended with huge morbidity and mortality.

When a woman develops life threatening complications such as peritonitis, septicemia, renal failure etc. consequent upon induced abortions she lands up in a regular secondary or tertiary care hospital where she is admitted and treated for these complications, and in case of death of the patient, certified to have died due to complications. The fact of criminal interference with her body is not recorded and invariably not reported".

Shri P.N. Saraswat, State Drug Controller, Rajasthan to whom notice of this petition was issued has stated in his reply that in the state of Rajasthan there is hardly any sale of the drug 'Mifepristone' across the counter and the drug is sold only on the prescription of registered gynaecologists. However, in some cases, namely, at one shop in the district of Banswara,, four shops in Kota, and two shops in Jhalawar district, it was found that this drug was being sold without the prescription of a gynaecologist and, therefore, in order to take action against these shops, show cause notices have been issued. These shops are:

1. Manoj Medical Store, Kota
2. Rajasthan Medical Agencies, Kota
3. K.V. Medical Hall, Kota
4. Gulati Pharma, Kota
5. Nagar General Store, Aklera
6. Vishnu Medical Store, Aklera
7. Doshi Medicals and General Store, Gangtalai (Banswara)

From this it appears that the Drug Controller has not been able to fully control the sale of 'Mifepristone' across the counter and there are a number of shops in the cities mentioned above where the drug is being freely sold.

The Drug Controller, Rajasthan has drawn the attention of the Commission to his letter of 14 February 2003 in which he has issued necessary directions to all District Drug Control Officers regarding three tablets namely:

1. टेबलट मिपेप्रिन: निर्माता मै. सन फार्मास्युटिकल इंडस्ट्रीज लि., बड़ौदा
2. टेबलट एम.टी.पिल: निर्माता मै. सिप्ला लि., पाठल गंगा, महाराष्ट्र
3. टेबलट फिजेस्ट: निर्माता मै. जाइडस एलीडेक लि., अहमदाबाद

He has further written in this letter as under:

उक्त औषधि 'टरमीनेशन ऑफ प्रेगनेन्सी' के लिये प्रेसक्राईब की जाती है, जिसे सिर्फ 'गायनोकोलोस्टि' के प्रेस्क्रीप्शन पर ही औषधि विक्रेताओं द्वारा बेचा जा सकता है।

अत: आप संबंधित औषधि विक्रेताओं की दुकानों का निरीक्षण कर यह सुनिश्चित करें, कि औषधि महानियत्रंक (भारत) द्वारा उक्त औषधि की बिक्री के लिये दिये गये निर्देशों की औषधि विक्रेताओं के विरूद्ध जांच कर नियमानुसार आवश्यक कार्यवाही कर, यह भी सुनिश्चित करें कि होल-सेल में चिकित्सकों अथवा नर्सिंग होम को उक्त औषधि की सप्लाई उनके लिखित आदेश प्राप्त करने के बाद ही की जा रही है।

The Drug Controller, Rajasthan contended that he has done all that was possible to prevent the sale of the aforesaid drugs across the counter without the prescription of a registered gynaecologist. The Commission is not satisfied with this assertion as mere issuing of instructions is not enough. The strict implementation of these instructions should have been assured with the full sense that the Drug Controller General of India in his instruction issued on 16 August 2002 had already stated that "Mifepristone" has already become "virtually over-the-counter-sale" in India although it is strictly meant for prescription sale.

Dr Kabra has also referred to Section 18 of the Drugs and Cosmetics Act, 1940 and has contended that there is a prohibition on manufacture and sale of certain drugs including any drug or cosmetic in contravention of any of the provisions of this section or any rule made hereunder. Dr Kabra has also invited our attention to Rule 106 of Drugs and cosmetics Rules, 1945 which is reproduced below:

"[106. Disease which a drug may not purport to prevent or cure:

1. No drug may purport or claim to prevent or cure or may convey to the intending user thereof any idea that it may prevent or cure, one or more of the disease or ailments specified in Schedule J.
2. No drug may purport or claim to procure or assist to procure, or may convey to the intending user thereof any idea that it may procure or assist to procure miscarriage in women.

In view of Rule 106 quoted above it is obvious that these drugs, namely, Mifepristone cannot claim by advertisement that they would cause miscarriage or abortion. But this aspect of the matter is of not much concern in the instant case where we are concerned primarily with the availability of these drugs across the counter.

The chemistry or the manner in which these drugs act on pregnant woman may now be seen.

Progesterone is a hormone secreted by the body that retains and sustains pregnancy. Mifepristone or RU-486 is a drug that antagonises the effect of progesterone secreted by the body. When administered to a pregnant woman, it stops the growth of pregnancy. The foetus, therefore, dies in the uterus. Misoprostol simulates the effect prostaglandin, which causes contraction of the uterus. When administered after Mifepristone, the uterus undergoes powerful contraction and expels the already dead foetus. It may be stated at this stage that the State Drug Controller has contended that "Misoprostol" is a drug for 'abdominal ulcers" as claimed by its manufacturers and, therefore, it can be freely sold. The Commission is not impressed. The literature of this drug containing instructions specifically contains a WARNING that this drug should not be taken by pregnant women as it may induce ABORTION. The use of this drug for termination of pregnancy thus cannot be ruled out as the manufacturers are themselves advertising it in a NEGATIVE way that this drug can be used for abortion.

Mifepristone has been approved for abortion (termination of pregnancy). This drug is approved under Drugs and Cosmetics Act exclusively for use as an abortifacient only. Misoprostol, in contrast, is approved as a prostaglandin analogue for several uses, especially as an anti-ulcer drug. It is contra-indicated in normal pregnancy. At the end of pregnancy, it is given to cause contraction of uterus to expel its contents.

The Drugs Controller of India has approved Mifepristone as abortifacient to be manufactured, marketed and sold with mandatory stipulations under the various provisions of Drugs and Cosmetics Act. Mifepristone is approved to be made available for Medical Termination of the Pregnancy (MTP) strictly under the provisions of Medical Termination of Pregnancy Act, 1971 (MTP Act). Under the MTP Act, pregnancy can be terminated by (1) approved physicians, (2) at approved centres, (3) for approved indications, and (4) for approved duration. The MTP Rules and MTP Regulations govern each of these four stipulations.

As per the aforesaid legal provisions, the doctors approved under the MTP Act alone can do MTP. All qualified physicians registered under MCI Act cannot do it. Only those who meet the stipulated approval criteria under the MTP Act can do it. It is only these approved doctors who can, under the law, prescribe and administer Mifepristone. Also, under the MTP Act, termination of pregnancy can be done at approved centres. The list of centres approved for MTP by the Director of Health Services is available with the Directorate of Health Services and a copy has been filed before the Commission.

Mifepristone is approved by the Drugs Controller of India to be prescribed and administered by the doctors approved under the MTP Act to terminate pregnancy at centres approved under the MTP Act. The pharmaceutical companies are to market the drugs in conformity of the MTP Act for which it has been specifically approved.

The pharmaceutical companies, however, are making it available at all drug stores and the drug stores, in their turn, sell it freely across the counter, or on the prescription of a registered medical practitioner, in contravention of the statutory stipulation that it can be sold for administration by a physician approved under the MTP Act and attached to and practicing MTP at an approved MTP centre.

Mifepristone-Misoprostol drug regime causes successful termination of pregnancy in 92-94 per cent of cases. In a percentage of failed cases, it causes severe bleeding which may prove fatal unless immediate surgical evacuation of the uterus is undertaken with or without blood transfusion support.

It is, therefore, mandatory that standby operation theatre and blood transfusion facility too should be available where medical termination of pregnancy is done by Mifepristone-Misoprostol method. In the absence of this a large number of woman may bleed to death at home. Presently 40-50 lakh abortions (MTPs) are done in the country of which 70 to 80 percent are early below 12 weeks abortions. This scenario with free, and frequently over-the-counter, sale of Mifepristone, especially in the towns and villages where recognised MTP centres are not available, is frightening. Neither are operative surgical facilities and blood transfusion facilities available for those who are under a threat to bleed severely consequent to unsuccessful administration of abortion drug regime.

Those who make available Mifepristone or Misoprostol to be administered in contravention of the provisions of the Drugs and Cosmetics Act and the MTP along with those who prescribe and administer it in contravention of the Acts are liable to be prosecuted under the provisions of the Indian Penal Code in addition to the provisions of the two Acts.

The State Drug Controller who is responsible for the implementation of the Drugs & Cosmetics Act and the Director of Health Services who is responsible for implementation of MTP Act, are individually and jointly responsible and competent to take action against the defaulters.

The Commission, therefore, recommends:

1. The State Government should ensure that free sale of Mifepristone preparations from drug stores on prescription of "ANY" registered medical practitioner be stopped as it is not only contrary to the mandatory stipulations imposed by the Drugs Controller of India. It is also wholly in violation of the provisions of MTP Act and the rules made there under.
2. State Drugs Controller be directed by the State Government to ensure by proper surveillance through Drug Inspectors that Mifepristone and Misoprostol are dispensed only on the prescription of the doctors approved for MTP who are attached to centres approved for MTP by the Director of Health Services so as to ensure that these drugs, namely, Mifepristone and Misoprostol are supplied only to the approved MTP centres and is not sold across the counter.
3. Those, including manufacturers, medical practitioners, retailers, who are found to be acting in contravention of the Drug & Cosmetic Act or the MTP Act, should be prosecuted by initiating appropriate criminal action against them.

7

Preventing Sex Selection/ Determination through PCPNDT Act, 1994

Selection or determination of sex of an unborn foetus has been a major social problem in India. This is done for many reasons, of which the most important ones are poverty and illiteracy. Before discussing the PCPNDT Act as a regulatory mechanism, we should understand what the terms 'sex selection' and 'sex determination' mean.

Sex selection: Selecting the sex of foetus. This is done by preconception separation of X sperm from Y sperm and then fertilizing the ovum with selected X or Y sperm.

Sex determination: Determination of the sex of already conceived foetus. This can be done by one of the three methods:

1. *Chorion villus biopsy:* This is done by passing a very thin catheter through the cervix of a pregnant uterus. The chorionic cells on the surface of the bag of water (amniotic sac) that surrounds the foetus are sucked out. The harvested cells are then stained (coloured) for X and Y chromosomes. The cells are then examined under a microscope for the stained X and Y chromosomes. If the cells stain for two X chromosomes the sex is female and when they stain for one X and one Y chromosome the sex of the foetus is male. Obviously, this test can be done only

after the amniotic sac is formed and is large enough to protect the foetus from injury by the catheter. The earliest stage at which it can be done safely is about 10 weeks of pregnancy. Even safer is in 12 to 14 weeks.

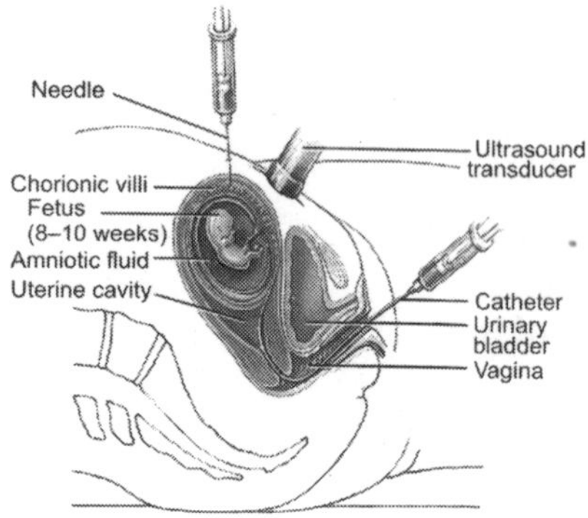

(b) Chorionic villi sampling (CVS)

2. *Amniocentesis:* In this procedure a needle is introduced under ultrasound guidance through the lower part of abdomen into the bag of waters surrounding the foetus. A small amount of amniotic fluid is removed. Cells in the amniotic fluid are separated. They are then stained for X and Y chromosomes as in chorionic biopsy samples and examined under microscope. Again, the procedure is unsafe before the 12th week of pregnancy.

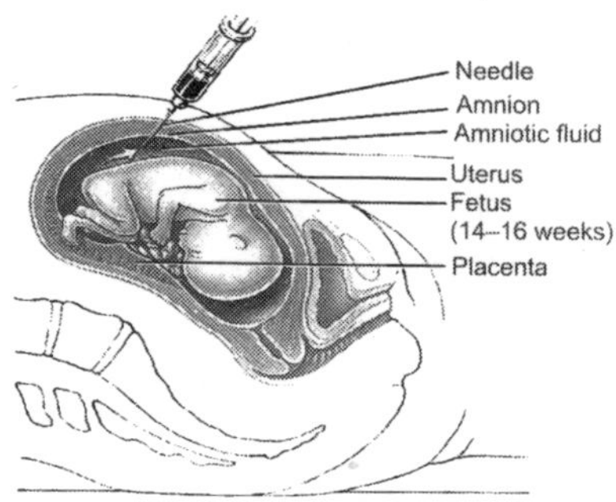

(a) Amniocentesis

3. *Sonography or ultrasound examination:* In this procedure cross-sectional images of the foetus are obtained. A vertical cross-section of the pelvis and thighs will pass through the external genitalia of the foetus. The external genitalia are sufficiently developed around the 14th week of pregnancy, the sex of foetus is not visible before this week. As the 20th week of pregnancy is the outer safe limit for MTP, sonography for sex-selective female foeticide is relevant only between the 14th and the 20th weeks of pregnancy.

Medically speaking, sex determination is indicated as a preliminary to excluding the diagnosis of hereditary diseases that are sex-linked such as Duchenne Muscular Dystrophy and Haemophilia A&B.

. During pregnancy ultrasonography should only be performed when indicated. The following is the representative list of indications for ultrasound during pregnancy:

- To diagnose intra-uterine and/or ectopic pregnancy and confirm viability.
- Estimation of gestational age (dating).]
- Detection of number of foetuses and their chorionicity.
- Suspected pregnancy with IUCD in-situ or suspected pregnancy following contraceptive failure/MTP failure.
- Vaginal bleeding/leaking.
- Follow-up of cases of abortion.
- Assessment of cervical canal and diameter of internal os.
- Discrepancy between uterine size and period of amenorrhoea.
- Any suspected adenexal or uterine pathology/abnormality.
- Detection of chromosomal abnormalities, foetal structural defects and other abnormalities and their follow-up.
- To evaluate foetal presentation and position.
- Assessment of liquor amnii.
- Preterm labour/preterm premature rupture of membranes.
- Evaluation of placental position, thickness, grading and abnormalities (placenta praevia, retroplacental haemorrhage, abnormal adherence etc.).
- Evaluation of umbilical cord – presentation, insertion, nuchal encirclement, number of vessels and presence of true knot.
- Evaluation of previous Caesarean Section scars.
- Evaluation of foetal growth parameters, foetal weight and foetal well-being.
- Colour flow mapping and duplex Doppler studies.

- Ultrasound guided procedures such as medical termination of pregnancy, external cephalic version etc., and their follow-up.
- Adjunct to diagnostic and therapeutic invasive interventions such as chorionic villus sampling (CVS), amniocenteses, foetal blood sampling, foetal skin biopsy, amnio-infusion, intrauterine infusion, placement of shunts etc.
- Observation of intra-partum events.
- Medical/surgical conditions complicating pregnancy.
- Research/scientific studies in recognised institutions.

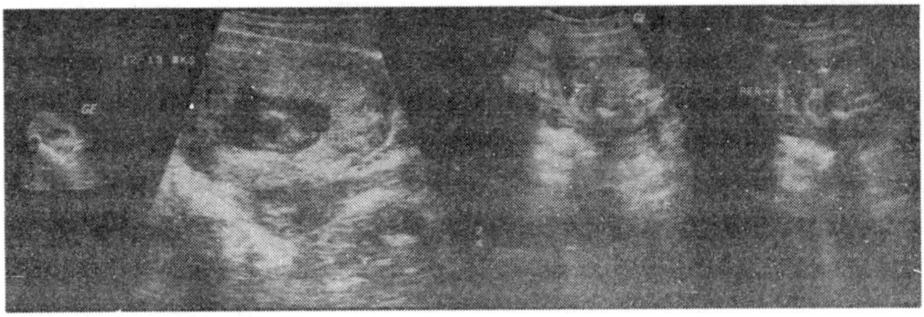

The person conducting ultrasonography on pregnant women shall keep complete record thereof in the clinic/centre in Form 'F' and any deficiency or inaccuracy found therein shall amount to contravention of provisions of section 5 or 6 of the Act, unless contrary is proved by the person conducting such ultrasonography.

It may be appreciated that while chorionic villus biopsy and amniocentesis are methods of genetic determination of sex, the sonography method is based on physical visualization of the tiny external genitalia of the foetus. However, sonography, being simpler and cheap, is currently widely used for sex determination. It is for this reason that sonography has been included in the Pre-Natal Diagnostic Techniques (PNDT) Act. Because of the significant prevalence of female foeticide in the country the entire focus has been shifted to this provision of the PNDT Act.

Pre-Natal Diagnostic Techniques (PNDT) Act, 1994

As per the 2011 Census in India, there were 940 females for every 1,000 males, which is a marginal increase from the 933 recorded at the 2001 census. But, the sex ratio in the age group 0–6 years has declined drastically from 945 in 1991 to 927 in 2001 and to 914 in 2011 – the lowest since independence. Decline to this great extent in the child sex ratio has sparked off an intense debate in political, legal, administrative and even academic circles as to how to contain this more vigorously in time to come. In India, the main reasons for the low child sex ratio are female infanticide, neglect of the girl child resulting in a higher female mortality at younger age, female foeticide, son preference, dowry, insecurity in old age, male bias in enumeration of the population and so on.

It is against this background that the PNDT Act was enacted in 1994 and came into operation with effect from 1 January 1996. To make it more comprehensive and stringent, it was amended in 2003 and is now known as Pre-Conception and Pre-Natal Diagnostic Techniques (PCPNDT) Act. It is aimed at:

- prohibiting sex selection before or after conception;
- regulating, though not denying, the use of pre-natal diagnostic techniques including ultrasonography for detecting genetic abnormalities or other sex linked disorders in the foetus; and
- allowing use of pre-natal diagnostic techniques including ultrasonography only at registered places and by qualified persons defined in the law.

Who are Liable Under the Act?

- Every person in charge of and responsible for the conduct of business of the unit providing pre-natal diagnostic techniques services.
- Persons who perform the tests.

- Mediator who is responsible for advising the pregnant women to the unit conducting determination of sex/sex selection.
- Husband/relatives of the pregnant women.
- The pregnant women herself is considered innocent under the Act, unless and until proved otherwise.
- Persons/units advertising about sex selection in any form.

Penalties Under the Act

- Imprisonment up to three years and fine up to Rs 10,000.
- For any subsequent offences, he/she may be imprisoned up to five years and fined up to Rs 50,000/100,000.
- The name of the registered medical practitioner is reported by the appropriate authority to the State Medical Council concerned for taking necessary action including suspension of the registration if the charges are framed by the court and till the case is disposed of.

Main Violations of the Act

- non-registration of centres/clinics;
- non-maintenance of records;
- communication/determination of sex of foetus; and
- advertisement about facilities for preconception/ pre-natal sex determination.

Cognizance of an Offence Under the Act

- No court shall take cognizance of an offence under the Act except on a complaint made by the appropriate authority.
- Investigating power under the Act rest with the appropriate authorities.

Difficulties Faced in the Implementation of the Act

- Invariably, the person seeking the illegal service, and the service provider, are both in agreement to defeat/circumvent the provisions of the law.
- Appropriate authorities (CMOs/Civil Surgeons) unable to devote adequate attention to this matter.

- Enforcing personnel do not have the necessary experience and expertise in legal matters.
- Slackness of enforcement in some states/UTs.
- Problem rooted in social behaviour and prejudices.

Consequences of Sex Selection

- 36 million less women as per 2001 census.
- Trafficking of women from economically backward/poor regions for marriage (e.g., West Bengal, Orissa, Madhya Pradesh, Bangladesh, etc.) and for the sex trade.
- Trafficking for sex trade/sex workers.
- Implications for HIV/AIDS/STI infections.
- Wife abandoned if son is not born.
- Increased violence against women. Abandoning girl child.
- Quacks giving *jadi-buttis* to have male child – deformed babies.
- Women undergoing repeated abortions to give birth to sons have implications for RCH (reproductive and child health), maternal mortality, physical health and mental health.

Thus, the Act prescribes a multi-tiered regulatory mechanism (Sections 7, 16A, 17, 17(5)). Regulating the stipulated facilities on the basis of prescribed technical grounds is simple and straight. This will ensure quality services for genetic and chromosomal screening and assisted reproduction methodologies. It will prevent presently prevalent excesses and gross exploitation in the field of assisted reproduction. Since foetal sex determination is done today by sonography only, regulating ultrasound facilities to prevent this misuse is a different proposition. Difficulties faced by those who sincerely wish to prevent foetal sex determination and prosecuting the delinquent sonologists, are very genuine.

Sonographic examination of pregnancy is very vital and common method resorted to for confirmation of pregnancy and continued well being and growth assessment of the foetus. Since it is a harmless and objective assessment, it is repeatedly prescribed as antenatal check up method.

Delinquent sonologists take advantage of this situation to offer and do foetal sex determination. The only way to prevent such misuse, to my mind, is to insist on the following:

1. Every licensed sonologist will maintain separate record of sonographic examination of pregnant women.
2. The record should include the obstetric history as communicated by the obstetrician (usually it is in form of 3 or 4 words) the duration of pregnancy and the result of sonography.
3. A photocopy of the record should be forwarded to the appropriate authority or to the nodal person designated by the authority.
4. Culling from the record all cases of 10 to 20 weeks of pregnancy should identify those where there was a possibility of foetal sex determination for possible foeticide.
5. All these cases or selected samples from them should be followed and results documented.
6. Only the presence of such a surveillance system can deter sonologists from misusing the technology.
7. Since the victim of such misuse – the pregnant lady – is an active partner, willing or coerced, the misuse will never be disclosed. Even when disclosed it will be difficult to prove.
8. An episodic sting operation to trap delinquent sonologists is *no substitute* for regular scrutiny, surveillance and monitoring.
9. There are sufficient provisions in the PNDT Act and its Rules and Regulations for the regulating authorities to evolve, and expect compliance from this proposed surveillance system (Sections 29, 30 & Rule 9).

As the foetal sex selection, determination and disclosure are penal offences under the PCPNDT Act, prevention of these offences by misuse of the medical technologies detailed in the Act is to be ensured by stringent implementation of the provisions of the PCPNDT Act.

Since, the offence of foeticide (and female foeticide) by illegal termination of pregnancy is committed in transgression of the provisions of the MTP Act. For prevention of female foeticide, therefore, provisions of the MTP Act and IPC have to be resorted to.

A strategy, invoking the various legal provisions, to prevent and punish the crime of foeticide and female foeticide is suggested hereunder.

The mandated monitoring and surveillance provisions in the PCPNDT and MTP Acts have to be strictly implemented and ensured.

Thus, medically speaking, the PCPNDT Act is an excellent piece of legislation. It is in the form of a detailed mandatory SOP (Standard Operative Procedure).

The PCPNDT Act seeks to regulate genetic and chromosomal screening to detect congenital anomalies or genetic defects and related activities thereto. In vitro fertilization and assisted reproduction activities are part of such activities. Access to facilities to ensures a defect-free conception is a reproductive right of a woman. Misuse of these facilities for sex selection and sex determination, enables and leads to sex selected abortions. The Act therefore, provides for preventing such misuse, essentially by declaring sex selection (Section 3A) and sex determination (Section 6) of the foetus a penal offence (Section 23).

This lesson is to provide critical insight into the provisions of the PCPNDT Act so that while ensuring reproductive rights of infertile and pregnant women, its misuse for sex selection, sex determination and sex disclosure is prevented. Delinquents amongst the facility providers are to be brought to book. Stiff penalties are now provided. However, while proceeding against the facility providers for technical deficiencies is easy under the amended Act, collecting proof of sex determination and disclosure by an ultrasound facility is a difficult proposition. Surprise regular checks by CMHOs of all licensed ultrasound facilities is more likely to deter delinquents than "sting" operations against a handful.

Strategies to Prevent Foeticide and Female Foeticide

1. Prevent seeking of second trimester abortion by making women aware of the dangers, undesirability and cruelty of second trimester abortion (right to information, personal autonomy, informed consent (IPC 88 & IPC 90).
2. Restrict availability of second trimester abortions for life threatening pregnancies only. (including rape induced pregnancies and congenital anomalies) by strict documented compliance of the MTP Act and Rules and IPC 312.
3. Monitor all second trimester terminations by receiving and verifying certifications (two) and consent form for every second trimester abortion (make doctors accountable for all second trimester abortions) as required under the MTP Act.
4. Monitor all second trimester sonographies as per the PCPNDT Act.
5. Conduct surprise visits to each approved MTP centre by the CMHO at least twice a year to verify records that are to be maintained as mandated by the MTP rules.
6. Conduct sting operations against suspected or reported delinquents.
7. Publish a list of all approved centres of first trimester and second trimester MTPs and encourage the public to report illegal centres undertaking MTP.
8. Prohibit termination of pregnancy beyond the 20th week without intimation and information to the CMHO (report to police? under CrPC 39 (v) read with Explanation 3 under IPC 299).
9. DMHS (Director of Medical and Health Services) to compile and submit annual report of all the MTP centres licensed and monitored by the CMHOs in the state.

(for the original text of the PCPNDT Act, 1994, see Appendices)

8

Female Foetal Loss and Gender Disparity

In the context of abortions, it is pertinent to discuss the issue of female foetal loss for the following reasons:

(a) There is a gender disparity in India favouring the male.
(b) There is a bias towards the female as exemplified by female infanticide, neglect of the girl child, heavy dowries to be given by the bride's parents and harassment (sometimes leading to so called dowry deaths) of the young wife by her in-laws. These are undeniable facts.
(c) Therefore, the natural assumption is that this bias manifests itself by culling of the female even before it is born ie female foeticide.

On seemingly scientific grounds, female foeticide is widely, almost universally, blamed for female foetal loss in India. This is based on presumptions that (a) the primary sex ratio (ratio at conception) will be equal unless distorted by medical intervention, (b) the secondary sex ratio (sex ratio at live birth) is bound to be equal unless foetuses of a particular sex are wilfully eliminated and prevented from being born, and (c) the gender ratio in the 0–6 year age group is just a continuation of the (permitted) secondary sex ratio at birth.

The case for female foeticide is sought to be strengthened by further arguments:

(a) Amniocentesis and chorion villus biopsy methodologies were used almost exclusively for foetal sex determination 80 per cent to 90 per cent of the time.

(b) Ultrasonography (USG) that replaced these methodologies is used for antenatal examination for the same purpose and to the same extent.

(c) Histochemical methodologies (through amniocentesis or chorion villous biopsy) and USG are equally efficacious methods for foetal sex determination.

(d) Every woman who opts for medical termination of pregnancy (MTP) after having undergone USG does so for a female foetus.

(e) USG can reveal the sex of a foetus at any stage of pregnancy.

Extrapolation of these perceptions to explain the emotive issue of gender disparity in the population has completely distorted the investigation of the problem. Female foetal loss, as evidenced by sex ratio at live birth in the country, is much more than is reflected in the sex ratio in the 0–6 age group and certainly much higher than can be accounted for by sex-determined female foeticides.

Female foetal loss, as revealed by the sex ratio at birth, is 100 to over 200 fewer females born per 1,000 males. It is too high to be accounted for by sex selective termination of female pregnancies alone. It has been present and prevalent in the country much before sex determination techniques came to the country. Even today, the female to male sex ratio at birth is much lower in rural areas than in urban areas where modern technologies are widely available. The trend analysis of the sex ratio at birth in rural and urban areas does not correlate with the increasing availability of USG. Over 75 per cent of the estimated four million abortions being done in the country today are in the first trimester of pregnancy, i.e., the period when sex determination is not possible by USG.

A critical evaluation of the available evidence for female foeticide shows how it has totally distorted the issue. An analysis of the sex ratio at birth in Rajasthan from 1974 to 2000 taken from the Data of Birth and Death Registry and correcting for under-registration and selective under-registration of female children clearly indicates the presence of causes *other* than female foeticide. The scientific literature elucidates possible causes of female foetal loss other than foeticide. It also documents well-substantiated studies that show female foetal loss may be due to sex-specific embryo toxins and foeto-toxins in the environment, toxins that are widespread in the Indian, and especially rural, environment.

There are, of course, studies to bolster the argument that female foeticide is a major cause of female foetal loss, but the findings are exaggerated and the inferences and conclusions not substantiated. Here are a few examples. Comments follow where indicated.

"... In one hospital, from June 1976 to June 1977, 700 individuals sought prenatal sex determination. Of these foetuses, 250 were determined to be male and 450 were female. While all of the male foetuses were kept to term, 430 of 450 female foetuses were aborted" (Miller 1985)" The Social Context of Sex Selection and the Politics of Abortion in India by Radhika Balkrishnan in *Power and Decision: The Social Control of Reproduction* (Cambridge: Harvard School of Public Health, 1994, p. 267).

Comment: The normal accepted primary sex ratio is 100 females to 105 males. A primary sex ratio of 250 males to 450 females is highly improbable and has not been reported even in studies of chemical disasters that exposed a large population to effects leading to a low male primary sex ratio from male foetal mortality. The article quotes no other figures or studies, is solely opinion/conjecture based and blames amniocentesis for sex selection.

"In order to convey the complex nature of the crises of sex selection I will describe an incident from a recent visit to India".

Comment: This is a purely anecdotal account, and follows a talk with an non-governmental organization representative.

"Female foeticide over the last 15 years has distorted sex ratios at birth in several Asian countries. Foetal sex determination clinics have been established in India over the last 20 years in northern and western cities. Presented here is the outcome of an intensive study of the abuse of prenatal diagnostic techniques for sex selection in rural population of 13,000 in Rohtak district. Parents tend to be calculative in choosing the sex of the next child and the decision is based on the birth order, sex sequence of previous children and number of sons. Transfer of reproductive technology to India is resulting in reinforcement of patriarchal values as professional medical organizations seem to be indifferent to ethical misconduct. ... The pregnancy outcomes reported by the women were 2,642 live born, 48 still births and 272 abortions (243 spontaneous and 29 induced). . .the aforesaid in a period of FIVE years. To reduce recall errors, we confined interviews to women who experienced a pregnancy outcome in the last five years rather than to all village women. There were 1,022 eligible women. The criterion of using pregnancy outcome in the last five years included almost all outcomes in the study villages in the recent past, as the average interval between successive births in Haryana is 28 months." ("Female Foeticide in Rural Haryana" by Sabu M. George and Ranbir S. Dahiya, *Economic and Political Weekly,* August 8, 1998, pp. 2191–2198).

Comment: Even if it is presumed that all 29 induced abortions (MTPs) in five years amongst the 1,022 study-eligible women of a total rural population of 13,000 were for female foetuses, the conclusions about female foeticide would be grossly exaggerated.

"India officially banned gender testing last year, but the practice is still common. A recent government study showed that of 8,000 abortions performed in one Bombay Hospital, only one was of a male foetus. Neighbourhood sonogram clinics crowd every city, and doctors take the machines on tours of countryside (sic)." (India's preference for boys tips sex ratio. September 17, 1995. Web posted at 12:36 a.m. EDT (0436 GMT), from correspondent Gayle Young, CNN, New Delhi, India, and quoted by Family Planning Association of India in its documents).

Comment: This is something scientifically unbelievable. How did the hospital do only female abortions? If it is to be concluded that the hospital was undertaking only female abortions after pre-natal sex determination, it may be noted that, let alone sonography, even amniocentesis and chorion villus biopsy do not enjoy such high accuracy (1 in 8000 failure rate). Even direct visualization of foetal genitalia by foetoscopy will not give such accurate results between 15 to 20 weeks of pregnancy, a period when the foetal genitalia are no larger than a grain of rice or wheat! External genitalia develop after 15 weeks and medical termination of pregnancy (MTP) is permitted upto 20 weeks. How did the hospital document the sex of the child in each case? How and where did they record it in the MTP register? If it was done for reasons of female foeticide and recorded as such, it is a criminal offence (of homicide), as MTP cannot be done for this purpose under the MTP Act.

"Fifteen years ago when the alarm was first sounded about the prenatal testing, the amniotic fluid was being extracted from the pregnant woman's womb and the chromosome pattern tested to determine the sex of the child. But now 95 per cent of the sex determination tests (SDTs) are by ultrasound equipment which has innumerable other medical uses and has mushroomed to small towns and even villages."

"According to evidence given to the select committee, between 1978 and 1982, 78(XX) female foetuses were aborted after sex determination and between 1986–87, 30 (XX) to 50 (XX) were aborted."

"Between 1982 to 1987 the number of clinics for sex determination increased from 10 to 248 in Bombay city alone."

"In 1986 government sponsored study in Bombay revealed that 84 per cent of the samples of doctors are performing amniocentesis for sex determination alone. Each of the doctors was doing on average 270 tests per month."

"(Conclusion) Between 1986–87 about 50,000 female foetuses were aborted after sex test" (Will bill to ban sex test control medical mercenaries: Usha Rai)."

Comments: The above conclusion is based on presumptions/conjectures:

(a) Since 95 per cent of amniocentesis examinations were done for prenatal sex determination, USG facilities that replaced amniocentesis were also similarly used and to the same extent.

(b) All ultrasound examinations in pregnant women are done for prenatal sex determination

(c) All post-ultrasound MTPs are for female foeticide.

Gender Disparity: Need to look beyond Female Foeticide

We have seen how exaggerated inferences about (sex-selected) female abortions and its projection as an exclusive cause of excessive female foetal loss totally distorts the issue of gender disparity in the population. Additional and larger causes of female foetal loss must be now be looked into and addressed.

Take the case of Rajasthan where gender disparity in the form of a lower F:M ratio has been present since the 1901 census. Social bias against the female child and female infanticide have been condemned, and over the last 100 years the overall F:M ratio has shown a sustained improvement Yet, selective female foeticide after prenatal sex determination has been considered as one of the causes responsible over the last 20 years to account for the low F:M ratio in the 0 to 6 year group in the latest census.

Though selective female foeticide (or on-demand abortion for the female conceptus) is an undeniable fact of life in India, especially in the urban and/or urban population, what has not been analysed and investigated is how far it is responsible, *if at all,* for gender disparity in the population.

Data from a leading private hospital of Jaipur helps place the situation in its proper perspective. In this hospital, of the children born alive, for every 1000 males there are about 830 females. Presuming that at conception the chance of the child being of either sex is equal, there has clearly been an excessive loss of female children in antenatal (pre birth) period. What is the cause of this? What selective factors operate against a female child in the womb causing excessive female foetal loss?

In this hospital, and substantiated by data cited in textbooks, spontaneous abortion, ectopic pregnancy, still-births and medical termination of pregnancy (MTP or induced abortion) are the causes of foetal loss during pregnancy. As compared to 80 foetuses lost per 1,000 live births due to natural causes, there were 65 foetuses/1,000 live births lost by MTP in this hospital. While evaluating the data from this fee-for-service private hospital catering to the relatively affluent population, the relatively better nutritional status and better antenatal care availed by this population has to be borne in mind. The rate of spontaneous abortion is much higher in the general population. Moreover, even in this hospital, it is only those cases of spontaneous abortion cases who develop complications that are admitted.

The predominant known cause of spontaneous abortions and stillbirth is a defective conceptus with fatal defects and anomalies. And amongst these congenital defects, neural tube defects (brain and its associated tissues) are predominant. Nature aborts these grossly defective foetuses early in pregnancy; others are either born dead (still birth) or born with defects, which later prove fatal.

A survey of primary data from the labour room register of Zanana Hospital and Mahila Chikitsalaya, the two maternity wings of SMS Medical College Hospital, Jaipur, for the period May 1992 to April 1993 (S.G. Kabra, Medicine Deranged, 1998) showed 724 stillbirths for 15,346 live births, i.e., 50 still births/1,000 live births. A.J. Babineau from North Carolina University, USA, after analysing the primary data of Zanana Hospital for a two-year period (1996 to 1998), reported 791 stillbirths for the 14,928 live births, i.e., 53 stillbirths/1,000 live births which is similar to that mentioned above. The stillbirth rate is exceptionally high, in fact 10 times the world average. The latest figures available for the year 1999 from Mahila Chikitsalaya reveal a stillbirth rate of 69/1,000 live births.

That the female child in the womb is selectively more vulnerable and sensitive to teratogenic (defect-causing) environmental insults is supported by the fact that, in the two aforesaid studies, from among the children born with neural tube defects (mostly brainless babies), 65 (Kabra's study) and 74 per cent (Babineau's study) were females. The two studies go on to estimate that, in Rajasthan alone, 8,000 brainless children are born dead or are born and die shortly after birth every year. Of these, over 5,000 are females. A high rate of neural tube defects have been also been reported from the states of Haryana and Punjab.

Finally, it is a well-known fact that a major cause, if not *the* major cause, of neural tube defects is a maternal nutritional deficiency of folic acid, a vitamin essential for brain tissue development. It is an eminently preventable cause of predominantly female foetal loss. There has to be a ready availability of folic acid around the time of (before, during and after, i.e., periconceptional) of conception. Since the brain is formed in the first six weeks of pregnancy, i.e., virtually before the pregnancy is confirmed, subsequent supplementation with iron-folic acid is useless in this regard. Other causes of prenatal foetal loss are to be investigated and corrected. It is high time that this be taken up as a national programme.

To terminate one's pregnancy by asking a doctor to induce abortion, i.e., abortion on demand under the MTP Act, is fundamental right of women recognized under Article 21 of the Constitution of India (protection of life and personal liberty) and codified in the MTP Act. The right of the child in the womb to survive under Article 21 is deemed subservient to the mother's right and is available to the child only in the later part of pregnancy. The legal provision to destroy the foetus by terminating a pregnancy is different from the provisions for therapeutic abortion under section 312 of the Indian Penal Code, i.e., terminating pregnancy on medical grounds to save the life of the mother. Though it is called medical termination of pregnancy (MTP), on-demand abortion for contraceptive failure is a non-therapeutic non-medical abortion. It cannot be called foeticide. A woman approaches a gynaecologist for termination of her pregnancy on the ground of contraceptive failure. The patient has not to disclose the sex of the child even if she has had it determined by ultrasonography. The doctor has no discretion or choice. In any case, the vast majority of on demand abortions are in the first trimester (first 12 weeks) of pregnancy where the sex of child cannot be determined by ultrasonography. To hold these first trimester abortions responsible for 'female foeticide' is untenable and deceptive.

Under the MTP Act, the right of on-demand abortion is extended to the 20th week on certification by two doctors. It is around the 15th week of pregnancy that the sex of the foetus can be determined by careful sonography, the presently prevalent and easily available mechanical method of sex determination. If the purpose of the lawmakers in granting the right of abortion was to recognize the fundamental right of women under Article 21, it could and should have been restricted to first 12 weeks of pregnancy. It would have automatically curtailed on-demand female foeticide. For rape induced pregnancy and congenital anomalies, therapeutic abortion was available under section 312 of the IPC. Ultrasonography is a powerful and essential diagnostic method in medicine. Its use cannot be restricted. The Prenatal Diagnostic Technique (Regulation and Prevention of Misuse) Act, which prohibits sex selection, determination and disclosure, cannot control termination, which is done under the MTP Act. Attempt to do so through the PNDT Act alone is doomed to failure. Ensuring strict compliance of the provisions of MTP Act and Rules and Regulations framed under it pertaining to the second trimester abortions is more likely to curb female foeticide.

The Demographics of Rajasthan as a Case in Point

The sex ratio in Rajasthan has always been unfavourable to women as per the census figures from 1901 to 2001. The factors responsible that have been operating all along to keep the F:M ratio low in the province and in the country are frequently interdependent and may be categorized as follows:

(a) Factors operating before conception, which affect x-bearing or y-bearing sperm or an ovum during spermatogenesis or oogenesis, and also during the fertilization process.
(b) Other factors which may selectively affect the foetuses of a particular sex after conception and during pregnancy.
(c) Post-birth factors that operate as gender specific life risks.

These factors are time, location and population-specific. Their elucidation therefore requires a time trend analysis for an extended period.

The sex ratio in Rajasthan as per the censuses from 1901 to 2001 is presented in Figure 1. It may be seen that the sex ratio of females per 1,000 males has always been low in Rajasthan where it has fluctuated between 905 in 1901 to 922 per thousand males in 2001, except for 1921 when it dipped to 896 per thousand males. It has thus gained, with low amplitude fluctuations, 17 points over the century, to reach 922 in 2001.

This is in contrast to the sex ratio of India as a whole, which registered a sustained fall from 972 in 1901 to 932 in 2001 with a very low amplitude fluctuation over the century.

Though the F:M ratio in Rajasthan has always been lower than the ratio for India, the difference has narrowed down to just 10 points (India 932, Rajasthan 922) in 2001 from a difference of 67 points in 1901 (India 972, Rajasthan 905). As a matter of fact, now rural Rajasthan equals the Indian average, having narrowed the gap of 74 points in 1901 (India 972, rural Rajasthan 898 females per 1000 males) to zero in 2001. Thus, the F: M ratio among the population (4.3 crore in 2001) of rural Rajasthan has registered a sustained improvement over the century, crossing the state average in 1961 and remaining above it since then.

The F:M ratio in the urban population of Rajasthan (1.3 crore in 2001) fell sharply from 947 in 1901 to 897 in 1921. Remaining approximately at the same level for next two decades, the F:M ratio rose sharply to 958 (gain of 61 points) in 1961. Conversely, the decade registered a very sharp fall of males in the urban population. More dramatic is the fall in the urban F:M ratio in the next decade (1951–1961) to 882 (a loss of 76 points). Urban Rajasthan has virtually never recovered from the two great falls of 1921 and 1961.

A multitude of social, economic, political, environmental and medical factors influence the sex ratio of the entire population. The determinants include postnatal and life long gender specific life risk and vulnerability, which are country, population and time specific. In the time trend analysis to ascertain causes for the low F:M ratio in the country, and more so in Rajasthan, it has to be borne in mind that the basic causes have been present all through the century; it is only the causes aggravating or improving the F:M ratio that need further elucidation. Partition and population migration in 1947, adoption of family planning as a state policy in 1953, legalisation of abortion-on-demand (MTP Act) in 1972, emergency and forced sterilizations in 1975–77 and introduction of prenatal sex determination technologies, especially ultrasonography, in the 1980s, are some of the direct impacting, relatively proximate factors that have not been adequately analysed. Certainly, to analyse the aforesaid changes in the sex ratio of the population of Rajasthan over the century, one has to look beyond sex selected female foeticide, a phenomenon in operation since 1980 only. How much has it contributed to the already operating causes of a low F:M ratio in the population?

To assess the impact of female foeticide, a more appropriate indicator should be the sex ratio at birth in the rural and urban population of Rajasthan, figures for which are available for the last quarter of a century. The sex ratio at birth reflects the prenatal factors that influence it.

Sex Ratio at Birth

The sex ratio for live births registered in Rajasthan is presented in Table 1 and Figure 2.

The figures reveal that, from approximately 1 lakh births registered in the rural areas of Rajasthan in 1974, the number of births registered in 2000 has risen to about 3 lakh. The F:M ratio of live births in rural Rajasthan that has always been less than 800 from 1976 to 1997 (except for 1981 when it was 817, because of a dramatic fall in the birth of live male children in that year), rose above 800 since 1998, with all time high of 825 in 1999. The fall in the number of births registered in the rural areas of Rajasthan from 1977 to 1983 follow the proximate consequence of forced mass sterilizations in the province.

In urban areas of Rajasthan, the number of live births registered has risen from about 60 thousand in 1974 to over 3 lakh in 2000. The F: M sex ratio of live births that had been above 850 from 1976 to 1999 (except in 1982 and 1987) fell below the 850 levels in 1990 and declined thereafter with a dramatic fall to 778 females per 1,000 males in 1993.

It is interesting to note that F:M ratio at birth in rural Rajasthan has always been lower by 30–100 points than that of urban Rajasthan, except in 1993 and 1999. The F:M ratio at birth for whole of Rajasthan has remained, throughout the period under study, in the vicinity of the baseline 1976 figure of 811, with low amplitude fluctuations, except in 1993 when it touched 781. A perusal of the trend analysis graph of sex-wise live births in Rajasthan from 1978 to 2000 reveals some interesting findings (Figure 2).

The fluctuations in the F:M ratio at birth over the years manifest as humps and troughs run parallel in the rural and the urban areas for 19 of the 25 years. In the internal migration of males from rural to urban areas the expected relationship is inverse. Interestingly, the urban/rural relationship in the sex ratio at birth is inverse in the years 1991 to 1993 and 1998 to 2000. However, the fall in the F:M ratio at birth in the urban areas registered a much steeper fall between 1991 and 1993 compared to the corresponding rise in the rural sex ratio at birth. The possible medical factors impacting during the aforesaid period under study were: mass forced vasectomies in 1975–76, aggressive family planning interventions after the 1981 census, sex selection technologies in the mid 80s, and yet-to-be elucidated factors in the 1990s.

Figures from a Private Hospital

For the impact study of modern reproductive technologies on the sex ratio at birth, long-term data from a modern city hospital are both interesting and relevant. The client population of such a hospital has had easy access and availability of the modern reproductive technologies that influence the sex ratio at birth. The Santokba Durlabhji Memorial Hospital is a 300 bed, fee-for-service, multidisciplinary, private hospital located in the centre of Jaipur. The proportion of females born is presented in Table 2 and its aggregate analysis in Table 3. The period under study is from 1972, when the hospital started functioning, to 2001, a period of 30 years. Till 2001, of a total of 23,933 infants born live in the hospital, 53.1 per cent were males and 46.9 per cent were females. The proportion of live born females was 53.3 per cent in 1972 and has steadily fallen to 45.6 per cent in 2001, with low amplitude fluctuations below the base line figure of 1972. It is interesting to note that in the early 1970s the sex proportion was favouring female births. From 53.3 per cent females in 1972, the female proportion remained above 50 per cent till 1980. The aggregate proportion of females for the period 1972 to 1980 of the 4,443 live born was 50.1 per cent. The sex proportion reversed in the period 1981–90 and of the 7,338 live births during this period, the aggregate proportion of females was 48.7 per cent.

The trend disfavouring female births continued through the next decade. In the period 1991–2000, the aggregate proportion of females was 44.5 per cent of the 10,809 live births at the hospital. In the year 2001, the proportion of females was 45.6 per cent females of the 1343 infants born live in that year.

It may be noted that it was in 1972 that abortion on demand was made available to the public by the MTP Act. It may also be seen that a reversal trend in the sex ratio at birth disfavouring females had started much before the sex selection technology became available to the public in the 1980s. The falling trend in the female sex proportion at birth continued during the decade ending 2000.

Seasonal Variation in Sex Ratio at Birth

The month-wise live birth data from the same hospital reveal interesting seasonal variations.

It may be seen that the most births in the 30-year aggregate of 23,933 births occur in the month of August. This holds good for the decadal aggregates of the 70s (9 years only), 80s and 90s and for the year 2001. The month of June favours birth of male children, which records the highest proportion of male births in the 3-decade aggregate, as well as in each individual decade. Conversely, the month of June maximally disfavours female births. The month of September appears to favour female births, the female proportion being highest in this month in the 3-decade aggregate; this holds good for the 70s and 80s but not for the 90s and the year 2001. Perhaps, to analyse the possible adverse impact of a particular season on the conceptus, the month of conception should be back calculated and analysed from the month of birth recorded.

Medical Termination of Pregnancy

It is alleged that the provisions of the MTP Act are being used for sex-selected female 'foeticide'. The right to terminate pregnancy is available till the 20th week of pregnancy under the MTP Act. This legally enables a woman to intrauterine sex selection of the foetus after the sex of the foetus is determined around or after the 15th week of pregnancy. The latter would be reflected in the number of second trimester abortions under the MTP Act. The figures for MTPs done before 12 weeks and between the 12th and 20th week are presented for

Rajasthan and India in Tables 4 and 5. It may be seen that over 80 per cent of the MTPs in Rajasthan and over 70 per cent in India have been undertaken before the 12th week of pregnancy from 1976 to 1997 for which trimester-wise data is available. Only 20 per cent to 30 per cent of all MTPs were done for pregnancies of 12–20 weeks duration. The increasing trend of sex-selected abortions, if present, would be reflected in second trimester abortions. The database covers over 96 lakh MTPs, spanning periods before and after sex determination technologies were available to the public. There is no evidence that the proportion of second trimester abortions is increasing over the years; also, the proportion shows no change before the availability of sex determination technology and after it.

Determinants of Sex Ratio at Birth

In 1988, Chahnazarian ("Determinants of the Sex Ratio at Birth: Review of Recent Literature", in *Social Biology* (1988; 35: 214–35)) reviewed the various factors that influence sex ratio at birth. The fact that more boys are born than girls (104–107 boys for every 100 girls) has been known since 1662. According to Chahnazarian, two kinds of factors determine the sex ratio at birth:

(a) those that determine the primary sex ratio, i.e., sex ratio at conception; and

(b) those that determine the survival of the embryo in the uterus:

The factors that determine the primary sex ratio, i.e., sex ratio at conception are:

(a) Y-bearing and X-bearing sperms, which may have different motilities or different survival times.

(b) The age of the ovum at fertilization.

(c) The chemical balance of the female genital tract.

(d) High levels of circulating gonadotrophins which may imply a lower sex ratio at birth as well as a higher rate of dizygotic twinning.

(e) The stage of the menstrual cycle. Male conception appears to be higher in early phase and later phase of the menstrual cycle.

(f) Coital rate. Women exposed to higher coital rates conceive earlier in the menstrual cycle, which may account for the greater number of boys born during wars.

The factors determining the survival of the embryo in the uterus are:

(a) The gestational month. Prenatal male mortality is reportedly highest between gestational months 3–5, lower between months 6–8, and higher again at term.

(b) Immunological interaction between mother and embryo, which may account for some sex selective spontaneous abortions.

(c) Three sociodemographic determinants of sex ratio at birth which are thought to be maternal age, paternal age and birth order.

(d) Socio-economic status. The prenatal mortality varies inversely with the socio-economic status, better socioeconomic conditions lowering prenatal mortality (and vice versa) in general. The effects of parental age, birth order, and parity are less clear.

(e) Race is also a factor, since the sex ratio (M:F)at birth for blacks is lower (102–104) than for whites (106).

(f) Fourteen univariate and 19 multivariate studies of effects of maternal age, paternal age, parity, birth order, race, and socioeconomic status on sex ratio at birth, with sample sizes in the millions from various countries have been analysed. More boys are born to younger parents, and lower order births have a higher proportion of males than do higher order births. In the multivariate analyses, when the effects of paternal and birth order are controlled, the effect of maternal age weakens, and the effect of paternal age appears to be stronger. The effect of birth order remains but is very small, and the effect of race persists independent of any effect of the other variables. Maternal age, parity, and birth order correlate positively with the proportion of male stillbirths. The results of the multivariate analyses show all of the effects to be very small, but that maternal age has no effect on sex ratio at birth; paternal age and birth order have a negative effect, and the racial effect persists independent of any other effect. The racial effect is clearly biologically determined at conception because blacks have higher levels of circulating gonadotropin and therefore a higher probability of conceiving girls. Parents in higher socio-economic classes are more likely to have sons, but the effect is largely due to the excess male mortality during most of the gestational period.

Environmental Factors

The changing sex ratio at birth has been a focus of recent research investigations throughout the world and a large number of published reports are available elucidating the factors that influence sex ratio at birth, documenting the havoc that pesticides and environmental pollutants are playing on the life in the womb. A whole lot of reproductive toxicants', 'endocrine disrupters', 'hormone disrupters', 'foeto-toxins' etc., in food chain and environment have been documented. The dismal situation in this context in India warrants urgent attention of those concerned with reproductive and child health in the country.

For example, Mocarelli and others have shown, in one study, that high levels of TCDD (tetrachlorodibenzo-p-dioxin, or, simply, dioxin) in serum samples of parents were linked to lower sex ratio (M:F)of their offspring. The study further showed that dioxin concentrations lower than that reported earlier might have similar effect if the father had been exposed. Further, male exposure to dioxin before and during puberty was linked to this sex-ratio effect, as seen by their offspring being predominantly female even though their offspring were conceived several years after the fathers exposure, when concentrations of dioxin in their serum samples were much lower.

The gap between the male and the F: M ratio at birth is wide and has been present since long. There is a need to look beyond the proximate 'female foeticide' presumption. The conspiracy of silence on the real causes of female foetal loss must end.

Female Foetal Loss

Study the given graphs and tables to evaluate female foetal loss by sex ratio at birth and possible determinants of female foetal loss.

Figure 1

Sex Ratio in India and Rajasthan, 1901–2001

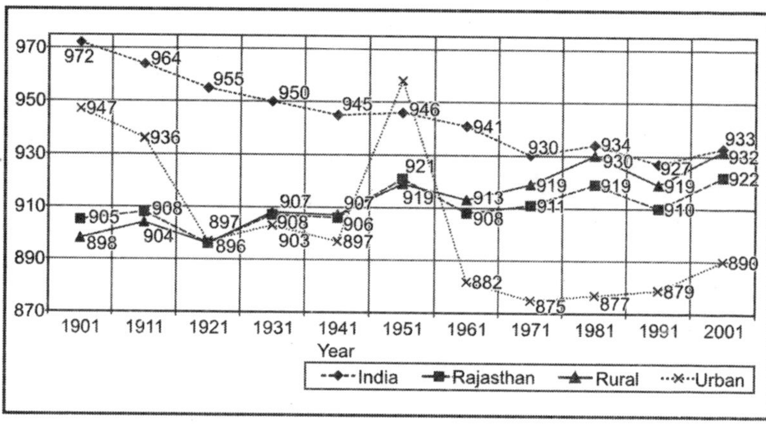

Table 2

Sex-wise Aggregate Live Births in SDMH

Year	*Total Male*	*% Male*	*Total Female*	*% Female*	*Total*
72–80	2210	49.7	2233	50.2	4443
81–90	3761	51.2	3577	48.7	7338
91–00	5999	55.5	4610	44.5	10,809
2001	730	54.3	613	45.6	1343

Sources: Birth and Death Registration Annual Report, 2000
Economics and Statistics Directorate, Rajasthan, Jaipur

Figure 2

Sex-wise Live Birth in Rajasthan

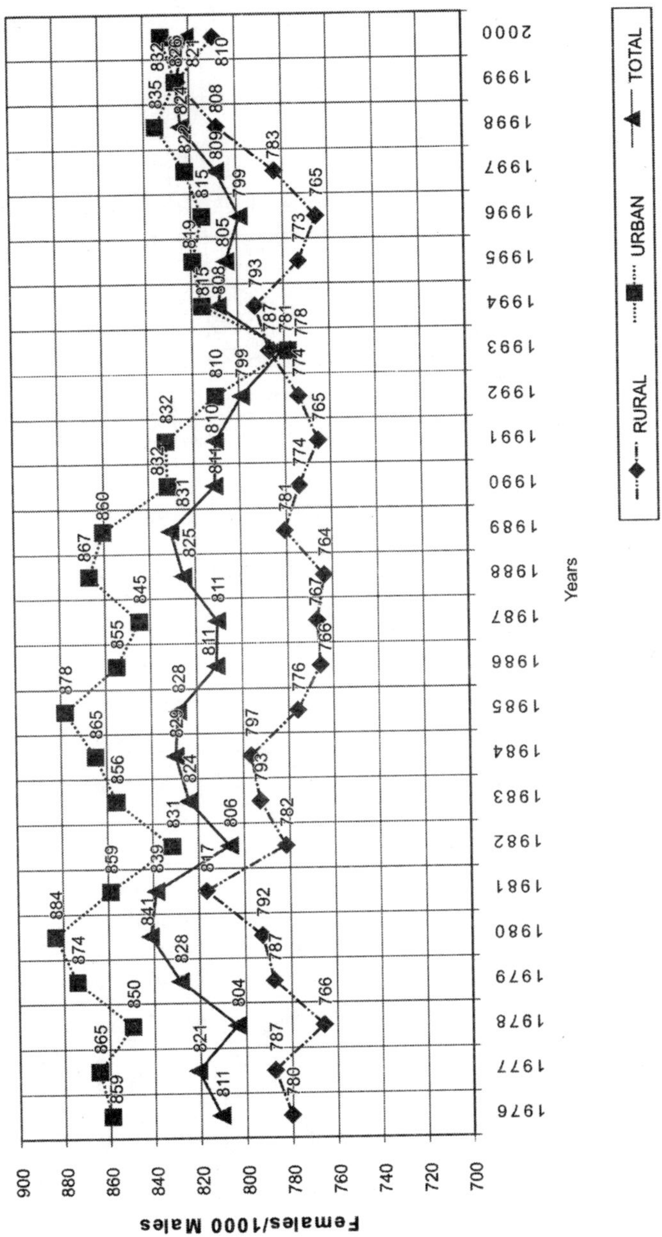

Table 1

Sex-wise Live Births in Rajasthan

	Rural				Urban				Total			
Year	Male	Female	Total	Females/ 1000 Males	Male	Female	Total	Females/ 1000 Males	Male	Female	Total	Females/ 1000 Males
1	2	3	4	5	6	7	8	9	10	11	12	13
1976	59,027	46,059	1,05,086	780	37,839	32,510	70,349	859	96,866	78,569	1,75,435	811
1977	48,544	38,228	86,772	787	37,266	32,219	69,485	865	85,810	70,447	1,56,257	821
1978	47,239	36,183	83,422	766	39,101	33,222	72,323	850	86,340	69,405	1,55,745	804
1979	44,952	35,396	80,348	787	40,492	35,386	75,878	874	85,444	70,782	1,56,226	828
1980	40,925	32,430	73,355	792	47,386	41,872	89,258	884	88,311	74,302	1,62,613	841
Total	2,40,687	1,88,296	4,28,983	782	2,02,084	1,75,209	3,77,293	867	4,42,771	3,63,505	8,06,276	821
1981	44,671	36,488	81,159	817	49,039	42,116	91,155	859	93,710	78,604	1,72,314	839
1982	51,875	40,550	92,425	782	50,834	42,267	93,101	831	1,02,709	82,817	1,85,526	806
1983	54,805	43,448	98,253	793	53,673	45,930	99,603	856	1,08,478	89,378	1,97,856	824
1984	59,644	47,510	1,07,154	797	55,528	48,025	1,03,553	865	1,15,172	95,535	2,10,707	829
1985	64,592	50,113	1,14,705	776	68,060	59,764	1,27,824	878	1,32,652	1,09,877	2,42,529	828
Total	2,75,587	2,18,109	4,93,696	791	2,77,134	2,38,102	5,15,236	859	5,52,721	4,56,211	10,08,932	825

Cont'd...

...Cont'd

1986	63,287	48,469	1,11,756	766	65,771	56,241	1,22,012	855	1,29,058	1,04,710	2,33,768	811
1987	63,885	49,000	1,12,885	767	81,846	69,146	1,50,992	845	1,45,731	1,18,146	2,63,877	811
1988	60,263	46,023	1,06,286	764	89,451	77,536	1,66,987	867	1,49,714	1,23,559	2,73,273	825
1989	57,867	45,183	1,03,050	781	97,010	83,466	1,80,476	860	1,54,877	1,28,649	2,83,526	831
1990	64,408	49,868	1,14,276	774	1,15,358	95,921	2,11,279	832	1,79,766	1,45,789	3,25,555	811
Total	3,09,710	2,38,543	5,48,253	770	4,49,436	3,82,310	8,31,746	851	7,59,146	6,20,853	13,79,999	818
1991	55,890	42,780	98,670	765	1,15,919	96,462	2,12,381	832	1,71,809	1,39,242	3,11,051	810
1992	55,334	42,823	98,157	774	1,22,051	98,878	2,20,929	810	1,77,385	1,41,701	3,19,086	799
1993	59,725	46,979	1,06,704	787	1,32,955	1,03,472	2,36,427	778	1,92,680	1,50,451	3,43,131	781
1994	57,960	45,934	1,03,894	793	1,30,552	1,06,464	2,37,016	815	1,88,512	1,52,398	3,40,910	808
1995	64,108	49,570	1,13,678	773	1,40,494	1,15,120	2,55,614	819	2,04,602	1,64,690	3,69,292	805
Total	2,93,017	2,28,086	5,21,103	778	6,41,971	5,20,396	11,62,367	811	9,34,988	7,48,482	16,83,470	801
1996	67,207	51,434	1,18,641	765	1,36,981	1,11,664	2,48,645	815	2,04,188	1,63,098	3,67,286	799
1997	81,766	64,053	1,45,819	783	1,53,218	1,26,010	2,79,228	822	2,34,984	1,90,063	4,25,047	809
1998	1,06,149	85,798	1,91,947	808	1,52,445	1,27,282	2,79,727	835	2,58,594	2,13,080	4,71,674	824
1999	1,15,655	95,446	2,11,101	825	1,71,246	1,41,458	3,12,704	826	2,86,901	2,36,904	5,23,805	826
2000	1,62,555	1,31,614	2,94,169	810	1,72,836	1,43,832	3,16,668	832	3,35,391	2,75,446	6,10,837	821
Total	5,33,332	4,28,345	9,61,677	803	7,86,726	6,50,246	14,36,972	827	13,20,058	10,78,591	23,98,649	817
Grand Total	16,52,333	13,01,379	29,53,712	788	23,57,351	19,66,263	43,23,614	834	40,09,684	32,67,642	72,77,326	815

Table 3

MTP Cases by Duration of Pregnancy in Rajasthan

Year	*Upto 12 Wks*		*12–20 Wks*		*NA*		*Total*
1976–77	5337	68.4	1045	13.4	1423	18.2	7805
1977–78	7202	86.9	1081	13.1	0	0.0	8283
1978–79	NA	NA	NA	NA	NA	NA	NA
1979–80	8966	86.7	1372	13.3	0	0.0	10,338
1980–81	10,044	87.3	1399	12.2	60	0.5	11,503
1981–82	10,414	89.0	1176	10.0	116	1.0	11,706
1982–83	11,416	89.3	1329	10.4	35	0.3	12,780
1983–84	12,840	88.3	1576	10.8	122	0.8	14,538
1984–85	13,428	91.3	1216	8.3	67	0.5	14,711
1985–86	14,995	89.6	1669	10.0	79	0.5	16,743
1986–87	15,623	90.0	1741	10.0	0	0.0	17,364
1987–88	17,857	89.6	2076	10.4	0	0.0	19,933
1988–89	17,999	90.3	1924	9.7	0	0.0	19,923
1989–90	20,938	91.1	2033	8.9	0	0.0	22,971
1990–91	21,194	87.3	3073	12.7	0	0.0	24,267
1991–92	23,680	100.0	0	0.0	0	0.0	23,680
1992–93	NA	NA	NA	NA	NA	NA	NA
1993–94	NA	NA	NA	NA	NA	NA	NA
1994–95	28,639	91.5	2658	8.5	0	0.0	31,297
1995–96	32,940	91.5	2890	8.0	155	0.4	35,985
Total	2,73,512	90.0	28,258	9.3	2057	0.7	3,03,827

Source: Year Books: Family Welfare Programme in India.

Table 4

MTP Cases by Duration of Pregnancy in India

Year	*Upto 12 Wks*		*12–20 Wks*		*NA*		*Total*
1976–77	1,89,403	70.1	52,770	19.5	28,194	10.4	2,70,367
1977–78	1,51,417	79.1	32,401	16.9	7514	3.9	1,91,332
1978–79	1,91,415	76.4	38,051	15.2	20,988	8.4	2,50,454
1979–80	2,78,112	80.3	49,805	14.4	18,410	5.3	3,46,327
1980–81	3,20,871	74.2	57,685	13.3	54,032	12.5	4,32,588
1981–82	2,92,634	81.9	47,744	13.4	16,882	4.7	3,57,260
1982–83	2,94,637	73.5	69,511	17.4	36,476	9.1	4,00,624
1983–84	3,72,211	75.5	57,238	11.6	63,247	12.8	4,92,696
1984–85	4,21,398	75.1	70,632	12.6	69,003	12.3	5,61,033
1985–86	4,27,495	75.3	71,029	12.5	68,983	12.2	5,67,507
1986–87	4,20,279	73.4	70,900	12.4	81,127	14.2	5,72,306
1987–88	4,44,502	78.7	84,017	14.9	36,384	6.4	5,64,903
1988–89	4,61,825	82.3	81,701	14.6	17,661	3.1	5,61,187
1989–90	4,52,461	76.2	95,715	16.1	45,484	7.7	5,93,660
1990–91	4,33,396	74.9	90,782	15.7	54,253	9.4	5,78,431
1991–92	4,70,216	74.5	75,413	11.9	85,512	13.5	6,31,141
1992–93	4,38,599	77.7	70,246	12.4	55,423	9.8	5,64,268
1993–94	3,71,960	79.2	64,269	13.7	33,361	7.1	4,69,590
1994–95	3,80,251	77.9	81,261	16.6	26,641	5.5	4,88,153
1995–96	2,71,614	84.9	36,989	11.6	11,349	3.5	3,19,952
1996–97	3,39,691	72.9	41,350	8.9	84,664	18.2	4,65,705
Total	74,24,387	76.7	13,39,509	13.8	9,15,588	9.5	96,79,484

Source: Year Books: Family Welfare Programme in India.

9

Modern Reproduction Techniques and Medical Ethics

Before discussing the modern reproduction techniques, such as assisted reproduction and tubectomy, in the light of medical ethics, we should understand what is *professional misconduct* or *infamous conduct* and how it is classified in medical profession.

In fact, professional misconduct is the behaviour outside the bounds of what is considered acceptable or worthy of its membership by the governing body of a profession. In medical profession, following activities come in the category of professional misconduct:

- Advertisement – soliciting patients in media, by large signboards or cutouts, or by improper, misleading advertisements.
- Association, i.e., associating with some one in a manner that would influence/effect professional judgment such as drug companies – gifts, laboratories – commission, colleagues – cut – back, employer – fee-splitting.
- Alcoholism.
- Adultery.
- Abortion – non-therapeutic abortions.
- Conviction by court for moral turpitude.
- Certificates – false, improper, misleading or of efficacy in modern medicine to unqualified persons.

- Contravention of Drugs Act.
- Breach of patients confidence.
- Operation without proper consent.
- Claiming to be specialist without recognized qualification or experience.

Medical Council Act

The basic law meant to regulate and maintain professional standards of the medical profession was the Indian Medical Act, 1956. However, in the zeal to encourage the 'Indian Systems of Medicines' and the 'Traditional Systems of Medicines', these essentially complementary systems have been projected and established as alternative systems of medicine. In the name of 'integrated medicine', a totally chaotic, unregulated and unregulatable free-for-all-system has come in to existence. Worse still, in the name of providing 'bare-foot doctors' for the suffering 'rural poor', anybody, irrespective of his/her basic qualification or capability, can get a legal license, after the so called "basic training", to practice as a Registered Medical Practitioner (RMP). An RMP, legally, can do anything and every thing that a regularly trained physician would do. And conversely, a trained doctor can do anything and everything as he chooses. There is no question of any norms, standards or ethics.

To place jaggery inside the cavity of the uterus to stop severe bleeding after child birth, is a criminal act for a doctor registered under the Medical Council Act, but would be a "life saving" act for a registered practitioner of Traditional Medicine. To instill anything unsterile in an eye after a cataract operation would be gross criminal negligence on the part of a modern ophthalmologist. But putting cow's urine after couching operation for cataract would be a fully justified procedure under the Indian System of Medicine. An acupuncturist is permitted to attempt to cure a cleft palate case by assuring the parents that electric stimulation from a needle "strategically" placed in the body will stimulate growth of tissues across the cleft, though, such an act, by others would attract penal provisions. In case of malignancies that are today identified as treatable or eminently controllable, not giving approved drug therapy would render a modern oncologist (cancer specialist) liable to legal action, but a practitioner of any other system of medicine claiming himself/herself to be a "cancer specialist" could give anything or deny anything to "cure" patients, without any consequence of law.

If acting beyond one's training, competence and skill is quackery, in India today we have virtually institutionalized quackery

Irrespective of which system of medicine one is trained in, including the self-training in the name of traditional medicine, one may do what appeals to his/her whim and fancy.

It is no wonder that the Medical Council of India and the other Medical Councils are non-effective and dead, as far as their function of regulating the standards of different systems of medicine is concerned.

Ethics of Assisted Reproduction

Artificial insemination or donor insemination.

Ethics and Morality

- The semen is collected by an unnatural act, that is, masturbation; is it ethical?
- Insemination is done by artificial means that is depositing the semen by a syringe in the vagina; is it ethical?
- Insemination from a person to whom the lady is not married; is it not adultery on part of both?

  It is not unethical because:

  - Masturbation is not associated with any harmful consequences.
  - As artificial insemination is done with the consent of the husband, it is not associated with adverse consequences of adultery, i.e., marital discord or violence, doubts about parentage of the child and disputes over inheritance.

It is not ethical in the following circumstances:

- In case of unmarried woman.
- When the donors are not medically screened for genetic defects, inheritable and infectious disease, RH-factor incompatibility and other disorders that may affect the foetus – a very widely prevalent situation in India.
- When the donors identity is concealed.
- When same donor is used in multiple cases in the same area.
- Where there is possibility of incestuous insemination.
- Where the source is a bank of frozen semen or frozen ova.
- Where it is a totally unregulated, unmonitored and unsupervised non-healing (non-professional) activity.

Adoption versus donor insemination by unmarried women – same question that are relevant ethical consideration for suitability of the parent for adoption, should be considered for donor insemination in single women, for the sake of the child.

Since artificial insemination in single woman is not undertaken to counter a defect in the husband, it does not constitute a medical indication, and hence, a non-professional act. Here, a woman desires to conceive without the physical contact needed to conceive – ethical for a doctor to undertake such a medically unindicated activity? is it not professionally debasing?

In-vitro Fertilization

Discard Problem

What should be done to the fertilized ova that remain unused?

- Is it ethical to use them without the consent of donor parents, or even with their consent, for the benefit of a third party?

- Is it ethical to destroy the unused ova without the consent of donor parents?
- Is it ethical to use the remaining fertilized ova for experimentation?

Risk to the Mother and Child

Risk to mother from hormone administration, laparoscopic operation, anaesthesia, and possibility of tubal pregnancy – have to be explained for an informed consent.

What about the unknown risks to the child?

Surrogate Mothers

Indications for surrogate motherhood:

- Ovulation normal (produces fertilizable ova) but can not bear child because of some defect in the reproductive system (ovum and sperm of the couple, womb surrogates).
- No fertilizable ova (husband's sperm, surrogate's ovum, artificial insemination, surrogate's womb)
- Informed consent of the surrogate mother:
    - Risks of pregnancy, its possible long-term health effects, even possibility of death must be considered before the surrogate consents to participate.
- Adoptive parents' contractual rights over the surrogate for the safety of the conceptus:
    - Can the contracting parents control the surrogate's activities that may damage the conceptus? e.g., restriction over smoking, alcohol consumption, drug intake etc.
    - What if the surrogate later wants to abort?
    - What about the parental right of the surrogate mother whose ovum has been used?

Ethics and Morals

- Payment to the surrogate is compensation for her services or is a purchase price for the child she bears?

- Contract: no payment if miscarries before four months; small compensation if miscarries after four months; must abort if foetus is found to be genetically defective; full payment for a healthy live child.

The contract conditions indicate that the price is for satisfactory product and is not a rental for the womb hired.

Is it ethical for a physician to participate professionally in such non-healing commercial transactions?

Is it ethical for a physician to submit a healthy woman, who desires to avoid pregnancy for its inconvenience, to unnecessary risk involved in the procedure of harvesting eggs from her body?

Is it ethical for a physician to participate where surrogate pregnancy is desired by adoptive parents for convenience and not for disabling medical indications?

Examples

Healthy single man or woman wants a baby to avoid emotional inconvenience associated with normal conception:

- Man asks for a surrogate mother
- Woman asks for donor insemination

Healthy woman wants a surrogate mother, as pregnancy would affect her career.

Non-therapeutic Abortion and Ethics

It is not unethical for a doctor to refuse to undertake a non-therapeutic abortion. It is unethical for a physician to advertise or propagate abortion.

Ethics of Assisted Reproduction: A Case Study

This case study highlights the gross human rights violations committed in experimental studies conducted for termination of pregnancy.

Human experiments are regularly and repeatedly conducted apparently without permission of the Drugs Controller or approval of a duly constituted ethical committee as per the guidelines of ICMR. Besides, these experimental studies are published by the official organ of the Federation of Obstetrics and Gynecology of India as research papers without verification of ethical norms. Cited hereunder are two such papers. Are such human experiments permissible, ethical and legal? Was prior permission of the regulatory authorities needed and granted?

> Prospective Comparative Evaluation of Intra-Amniotic Versus Extra-Amniotic Routes for Ethacridine Lactate for Second Trimester MTP: by Pankaj Desai and Purvi Patel, Dept. of Obst. & Gyn., Medical College & S.S.G. Hospital, Vadodara, published in *J. of Obst. & Gyn. of India,* Vol. 51, No.6: November/December 2001, pp. 158–160.

This study has been carried out to determine whether the intra-amniotic route of instillation of ethacridine lactate was superior to extra-amniotic route of instillation for second trimester medical termination of pregnancy (MTP). This was prospective comparative study of women between 14 and 20 weeks of gestation admitted for pregnancy termination. Pregnancy termination was done in 100 women each by intra-amniotic and extra-amniotic route. There was no difference in the overall success rate. There was an insignificant decrease in mean instillation abortion interval (35.7 hours versus 38.5 hours).

Cohen first described the use of the Ethacridine lactate by extra-amniotic route for termination of second trimester pregnancy in 1946 (Marett 1998). (this citation is not in the bibliography of references. Also in 1996 article in the same journal Cohen is cited for 1846 – there also without reference.). Since then, it has been conventionally used for second trimester pregnancy termination by extra-amniotic route. (Why a repeat human expt. after 55 years?) However, this procedure has its drawbacks in the form of a longer instillation-abortion interval, a higher incidence of incomplete abortion and more chances of the foetus being born alive. (It hurts the good doctors' sensibilities to receive a living child in the hands and then having to dump it in the bucket – a doctor dumping a living child in the bucket to die. The doctors, therefore, wish to be merciful by instilling the killing substance directly in contact with the body of the foetus so that it is slaughtered inside the womb and not after it leaves it. Unfortunately, it appears from the results that they have not succeeded in their merciful endeavour.)

Note: Ethacridine lactate is an antiseptic chemical for topical use. How, why and on what medical basis it was used as abortificient by intra-uterine instillation is not available in the pharmacology text books. None of the approved pharmacopoeias, viz., Indian, British, USA, USSR or European pharmacopoeias include it for abortion. It is marketed by three Indian pharmaceutical companies, presumably on approval of the Central Drugs Controller, under Japanese pharmacopoeia. The drug insert states that it is an antiseptic that on extra-amniotic instillation causes abortion by (1) mechanical stimulation of uterus, and (2) by damaging decidual lysosomes which leads to synthesis and release of prostaglandins. The later, it may be noted, occurs with any substance that cause cellular damage and is not specific to ethacridine. On what specific chemical action it has been approved as abortificent is not known. In any case it is approved for extra-amniotic instillation. It cannot be used for intra-amniotic instillation. If some one wishes to undertake human experiments (drug trial) with intra-amniotic instillation she/he has to take prior approval of the Drugs Controller under Schedule 'Y' of the Drugs and Cosmetics Act. Even instillation of distilled water and saline has been found to be dangerous on intra-amniotic route resulting in maternal deaths. There is no rationality for the use of ethacridine lactate – an anti-septic chemical – for intra-amniotic instillation. Drugs Controller cannot grant permission for it unless prior animal experiments have established its rationale and safety. How does ICMR permit such direct and potentially dangerous human experiment?

In the same context, how can an experimenter (human experiments) be permitted or allowed to use a 'powdered tablet' for intra-uterine instillation and that too in conjunction with a noxious antiseptic chemical? as has been done in the under mentioned study report.

Arun H. Nayak, Bhavana P. Shah and Chandni M. Alwani (1996). Extra-amniotic Instillation of Tablet Primprost with Ethacridine Lactate for Termination of Second Trimester Pregnancy, *J. of Obst. & Gyn. of India,* Vol. 46:753–758.

These are just two examples. Large number of such experimental studies are going on in the field of contraception and medical termination of pregnancy. A cell has to be opened for monitoring such experiments/trials in the field of reproduction. Medical institutions may be required to intimate about such trials under the Right to Information Act.

Transgression of Quality Services for Tubectomies etc., apropos Medical Ethics: A Case Study

Nuremberg Trial: Experiments and Experimenters Then and Now

The following experiments conducted by Nazi medical men on inmates of concentration camps illustrate the then adopted attitudes of those medical men.

1. A young woman is selected. Young and a woman, because she has the required amount of subcutaneous fat. She is shot in the calf to create a ragged wound. Contaminated dust from the street is thrown into the wound to induce gas gangrene. She is given the trial medicine to test if it is effective.
2. An inmate is selected. His hands are tied at the back. His head is dipped in a bucket full of cold seawater, till he chokes. This is to simulate drowning of pilots bailing out of planes shot over the seas. An attempt is then made to resuscitate the inmate.

   Also, an inmate is selected and his body is immersed in ice-cold seawater to assess the effect of such exposure on the body, and the time duration of tolerance of such exposure.

3. An inmate is selected. He is put in the gear of a pilot. He is put in a compression chamber to simulate conditions inside an aircraft at high altitudes. The chamber is than suddenly decompressed to simulate the atmospheric conditions to which a pilot would be exposed when his plane is shot at a high altitude. Conditions of free fall through the air are simulated.
4. A young male inmate is selected. His testicles are exposed to various doses of X-ray radiation. The sensitive gonadal cells are expected to be destroyed by such exposure, rendering the person sterile. The experiment is to implement the eugenic and genetic policy of the state to improve the quality of the German race. Excessive exposure would lead to gangrene and sloughing of the scrotum and the testes along with serious systemic ill effects.

Answers of Doctors at the Nuremberg Trial

When asked at the Nuremberg trial, why they had conducted such non-therapeutic, unethical and inhuman experiments, the concerned medical men gave the following answers:

1. These were the orders of the state – what could I do? (the perpetrators posing as victims).
2. It was for the larger good of the society and the patients (professed beneficence and paternalism).
3. How does it matter? They were conducted on persons of inferior races. In any case, they had all been condemned by the state to death (self-righteous arrogance).

The Indian Scenario

1. Participation of doctors in the forced sterilization drive during the emergency. (Ethics of 'Association')
2. Participation of doctors in sterilization camps under unacceptable surgical norms and conditions. (Ethics of 'Non-malfeasance')
3. Participation in non-therapeutic interventions at the dictates of the state. (Ethics of 'Professional Code of Conduct and Aggressive Paternalism')

4. Conducting research on humans, especially for induced abortions and female sterilizations, without informed consent and approved scientific protocols. (Ethics of 'Informed Consent, Patient Autonomy and Professional Conduct')

Answers of the Indian Doctors

1. What can we do? We are government servants; we have to carry out the orders of the government. If we do not, we are penalized.
2. It may be excessive, but what is done is for the larger good of the society and the country. To participate in nation-building is our duty.
3. Informed consent, medical standards and ethics are impractical niceties for the type of persons we deal with. Poor, illiterate and rustic, they do not know what is good for them. Adhering to such niceties, you cannot do anything on them. In any case, accustomed to live in sub-standard conditions, they have great natural resistance.

Medical Ethics: Abortion

Abortion = expulsion or removal or killing of a non-viable embryo or foetus.

Miscarriage = same as above in a viable foetus.

Since, at what stage a conceptus should be considered viable is not uniformly agreed upon, there is considerable overlap between the two terms – abortion and miscarriage.

If and at what stage the foetus is a person?

Does it have inherent or attributed rights?

The right of the foetus as a person and the right of privacy and control over her body of the mother?

Foetus as an alien invader?

Who has a Right to Life?

- Species Principle: All those that are (a) conceived of humans, (b) born of humans, or (c) genetically human, have a right to life.

- Potentiality Principle: All those that potentially possess or will possess in due course of time distinctly human characteristics, have a right to live.
- Present Enjoyment Principle: All those who currently possess distinctly human characteristics, have a right to live.

Wedge argument	Make an exception and the door is opened for abuses.
Foetus's right to life	A foetus has serious, though not absolute right to life.
Right of woman over her body	A pregnant woman has serious, but not absolute right over her body apropos the foetus.
Right of foetus	Right to live.
Right of pregnant mother	Right to privacy or non-interference. Right to life and right not to have her health destroyed. Right to abort. Right to select sex of the child. Right to avoid birth of a defective child.
Right of the State	Interest of the state in the health of mother. Interest of the state in the life of the foetus.

The right of the state to eliminate foetuses or to prevent children being borne alive is fabricated and has no genuine constitutional foundation.

Impact of such a right being exercised by the state on human dignity, human values and social ethos? Right of society to human dignity?

Therapeutic Abortions and Non-therapeutic Abortions

Therapeutic abortions:	When continuation of pregnancy threatens mother's life. When it threatens the mother's health. When the foetus has a serious congenital defect. When the pregnancy is a result of rape or incest.
Non-therapeutic abortion:	Abortions sought for pregnancy due to contraceptive failure Abortions sought for mother's convenience, career, social stigma or poverty. Abortions to choose the sex of the child. Abortions to limit the family size.

Social eugenics often includes racism of worst form. WHO supported MTP programme (courtesy: western countries) as means of population control in India in the name of welfare reform, is an example.

Moral and Ethical Issues

- Some of the non-therapeutic abortions are now legally permissible, but are not ethical. A physician has a right to refuse them. Ethics of such abortions should be considered before a physician undertakes a non-therapeutic abortion.
- Since abortion in late pregnancy is risky for the mother, should not the non-therapeutic abortions be restricted to 12 weeks of pregnancy? The MTP Act recognizes such enhanced risk.
- Is it ethical to permit, undertake or overlook abortions in contravention of the safety provisions of the MTP Act?
- Is it ethical, moral or constitutional for the state to enact laws or frame rules that would coerce the couple to undertake termination of pregnancy? e.g., denial of government job, post, perks or facilities if a person allows birth of a third child.

Appendices

Appendix I
The Medical Termination of Pregnancy Act, 1971

An Act to provide for the termination of certain pregnancies by Registered Medical Practitioners and for matters connected therewith or incidental thereto.

Be it enacted by Parliament in the Twenty-second Year of the Republic of India as follows:

1. Short title, extent and commencement:
   (1) This Act may be called the Medical Termination of Pregnancy Act, 1971.
   (2) It extends to the whole of India except the State of Jammu and Kashmir.
   (3) It shall come into force on such date as the Central Government may, by notification in the Official Gazette, appoint.
2. Definitions: In this Act, unless the context otherwise requires,
   (a) "guardian" means a person having the care of the person of a minor or a mentally ill person (substituted);
   (b) "mentally ill person" means a person who is in need of treatment by reason of any mental disorder other than mental retardation (substituted);
   (c) "minor" means a person who, under the provisions of the Indian Majority Act, 1875 (9 of 1875), is to be deemed not to have attained his majority;

(d) "registered medical practitioner" means a medical practitioner who possesses any recognized medical qualification as defined in clause (h) of section 2 of the Indian Medical Council Act, 1956, (102 of 1956), whose name has been entered in a State Medical Register and who has such experience or training in gynaecology and obstetrics as may be prescribed by rules made under this Act.

3. When pregnancies may be terminated by registered medical practitioners:

(1) Notwithstanding anything contained in the Indian Penal Code (45 of 1860), a registered medical practitioner shall not be guilty of any offence under that Code or under any other law for the time being in force, if any pregnancy is terminated by him in accordance with the provisions of this Act.

(2) Subject to the provisions of sub-section (4), a pregnancy may be terminated by a registered medical practitioner,

(a) Where the length of the pregnancy does not exceed twelve weeks if such medical practitioner is, or

(b) Where the length of the pregnancy exceeds twelve weeks but does not exceed twenty weeks, if not less than two registered medical practitioner are, of opinion, formed in good faith, that

(i) the continuance of the pregnancy would involve a risk to the life of the pregnant woman or of grave injury to her physical or mental health; or

(ii) there is a substantial risk that if the child were born, it would suffer from such physical or mental abnormalities to be seriously handicapped.

Explanation 1. Where any pregnancy is alleged by the pregnant woman to have been caused by rape, the anguish caused by such pregnancy shall be presumed to constitute a grave injury to the mental health of the pregnant woman.

Explanation 2. Where any pregnancy occurs as a result of failure of any device or method used by any married woman or her husband for the purpose of limiting the number of children, the anguish caused by such unwanted pregnancy may be resumed to constitute a grave injury to the mental health of the pregnant woman.

(3) In determining whether the continuance of a pregnancy would involve such risk of injury to the health as is mentioned in sub-section (2), account may be taken of the pregnant women's actual or reasonable foreseeable environment.

(4) (a) No pregnancy of a woman, who has not attained the age of eighteen years, or, who, having attained the age of eighteen years, is a mentally ill person, (substituted) shall be terminated except with the consent in writing of her guardian.

(b) Save as otherwise provided in clause (a), no pregnancy shall be terminated except with the consent of the pregnant woman.

4. Place where pregnancy may be terminated: No termination of pregnancy shall be made in accordance with this Act at any place other than

(a) a hospital established or maintained by Government, or

(b) a place for the time being approved for the purpose of this Act by Government or a District Level Committee constituted by that Government with the Chief Medical Officer or District Health Officer as the Chairperson of the said Committee (substituted)

5. Sections 3 and 4 when not to apply:

(1) The provisions of section 4, and so much of the provisions of sub-section (2) of section 3 as relate to the length of the pregnancy and the opinion of not

less than two registered medical practitioners, shall not apply to the termination of a pregnancy by a registered medical practitioner in a case where he is of opinion, formed in good faith, that he termination of such pregnancy is immediately necessary to save the life of the pregnant woman.

(2) Notwithstanding anything contained in the Indian Penal Code (45 of 1860), the termination of a pregnancy by a person who is not a registered medical practitioner shall be an offence punishable with rigorous imprisonment of a term which shall not be less than two years but which may extend to seven years under that Code, and that shall to this extent, stand modified (substituted).

(3) Whoever terminates any pregnancy in a place other than that mentioned in section 4, shall be punishable with rigorous imprisonment for a term which shall not be less than two years but which may extend to seven years (substituted).

(4) Any person being owner of a place which is not approved under clause (b) of section 4 shall be punishable with rigorous imprisonment for a term which shall not be less than two years but which may extend to seven years. (substituted).

Explanation 1. For the purpose of this section, the expression "owner" in relation to a place means any person who is the administrative head or otherwise responsible for the working or maintenance of a hospital or place, by whatever name called, where the pregnancy may be terminated under this Act. (substituted)

Explanation 2. For the purposes of this section, so much of the provisions of clause (d) of section (2) as relate to the possession, by a registered medical practitioner, of experience or training in gynaecology and obstetrics shall not apply.

6. Power to make rules:
   (1) The Central Government may, by notification in the Official Gazette, make rules to carry out the provisions of this Act.
   (2) In particular, and without prejudice to the generality of the foregoing power, such rules may provide for all or any of the following matters, namely:
      (a) the experience or training, or both, which is registered medical practitioner shall have if he intends to terminate any pregnancy under this Act; and
      (b) such other matters as are required to be or may be, provided by rules made under this Act.
   (3) Every rule made by the Central Government under this Act shall be laid, as soon as may be after it is made, before each House of Parliament while it is in session for a total period of thirty days which may be comprised in one session or in two successive sessions, and if, before the expiry of the session in which it is so laid or the session immediately following, both Houses agree in making any modification in the rule or both Houses agree that the rule should not be made, the rule shall thereafter have effect only in such modified form or be of no effect, as the case may be; so, however, that any such modification or annulment shall be without prejudice to the validity of anything previously done under that rule.
7. Power to make regulations:
   (1) The State Government may, by regulations
      (a) require any such opinion as is referred to in sub-section (2) of section 3 to be certified by a registered medical practitioner or practitioners concerned, in such form and at such time as may be specified in such regulations, and the preservation or disposal of such certificates;
      (b) require any registered medical practitioner, who terminates a pregnancy, to give intimation

of such termination and such other information relating to the termination as may be specified in such regulations;

(c) prohibit the disclosure, except to such purposes as may be specified in such regulations, of intimations given or information furnished in pursuance of such regulations.

(2) The intimation given and the information furnished in pursuance of regulations made by virtue of clause (b) of sub-section (1) shall be given or furnished, as the case may be, to the Chief Medical Officer of the State.

(3) Any person who willfully contravenes or willfully fails to comply with the requirements of any regulation made under sub-section (1) shall be liable to be punished with fine, which may extend to one thousand rupees.

8. Protection of action taken in good faith:

No suit or legal proceedings shall lie against any registered medical practitioner for any damage caused or likely to be caused by anything, which is in good faith done or intended to be done under this Act.

Thus, in addition to therapeutic abortion, non-therapeutic second trimester abortion from 13 to 20 weeks is permitted under Section 3 sub-section 2(a) read with Explanation 2, giving a liberal interpretation to Explanation 2 for family planning programme of the state.

The basic question that begs is whether it is proper to permit second trimester termination of pregnancy for contraceptive failure for family planning measures? Should it not be restricted to the first trimester (12 weeks) under the MTP Act? Therapeutic abortions, when the continuation of pregnancy threatens the life of mother, may continue to be done under Section 312 of IPC following a due process to terminate a life. Incidentally, this will prevent female foeticide also as foetal sex is determinable by ultrasound only after 14–15 weeks. IPC 312. Whoever voluntarily causes a woman with child to miscarry shall, if such miscarriage be not caused in good faith for the purpose of saving the life of the woman, be punished with imprisonment of either description for a term which may extend to three years, or with fine, or with both; and, if the woman be quick with child, shall be punished with imprisonment of either description for a term which may extend to seven years, and shall also be liable to fine.

Explanation a woman who causes herself to miscarry, is within the meaning of this section.

Article 21 of the Constitution of India: Protection of Life and Personal Library:

No person shall be deprived of his life and personal liberty except according to procedure established by law.

The right of woman to life when a foetus threatens the life of the mother is to be available under Section 312 IPC and right to personal liberty not to continue the pregnancy caused due to contraceptive failure be restricted to 12 weeks of pregnancy under the MTP Act.

Appendix II
Medical Termination of Pregnancy Regulations, 2003

Introduction

G.S.R. 486 (E): In exercise of powers conferred by section 7 of the Medical Termination of Pregnancy Act, 1971 (34 of 1971), the Central Government hereby makes the following regulations, namely;

1. Short title, extent and commencement:
   (1) These regulations may be called the Medical Termination of Pregnancy Regulations, 2003.
   (2) They extend to all the Union Territories.
   (3) They shall come into force on the date of their publication in the Official Gazette.
2. Definitions: In these regulations, unless the context otherwise requires,
   (a) "Act" means the Medical Termination of Pregnancy Act, 1971 (34 of 1971);
   (b) "Admission Register" means the register maintained under regulation 5;
   (c) Chief Medical Officer of the District means the Chief Medical Officer of the District by whatever name called;
   (d) "Form" means a form appended to these regulations;
   (e) "hospital" means a hospital established or maintained by the Central Government or the Government of Union territory;
   (f) "section" means a section of the Act.
3. Form of certifying opinion or opinions:
   (1) Where one registered medical practitioner forms or not less than two registered medical practitioners form such opinion as is referred to in sub section (2) of section 3 or 5, he or she shall certify such opinion in Form I.

(2) Every registered medical practitioner who terminates any pregnancy shall, within three hours from the termination of the pregnancy certify such termination in Form I.

4. Custody of forms:

(1) The consent given by a pregnant woman for the termination of her pregnancy, together with the certified opinion recorded under section 3 oR section 5, as the case may be and the intimation of termination of pregnancy shall be placed in an envelope which shall be sealed by the registered medical practitioner or practitioners by whom such termination of pregnancy was performed and until that envelope is sent to the head of the hospital or owner of the approved place or the Chief Medical Officer of the State, it shall be kept in the safe custody of he concerned registered medical practitioner or practitioners, as the case may be.

(2) On every envelope referred to in sub-regulation (1), pertaining to the termination of pregnancy under section 3, there shall be noted the serial number assigned to the pregnant woman in the Admission Register and the name of the registered medical practitioner or practitioners by whom the pregnancy was terminated and such envelope shall be marked "SECRET".

(3) Every envelope referred to in sub-regulation (2) shall be sent immediately after the termination of the pregnancy to the head of the hospitai or owner of the approved place where the pregnancy was terminated.

(4) On receipt of the envelope referred to in sub-regulation (3), the head of the hospital or owner of the approved place shall arrange to keep the same in safe custody.

(5) Every head of the hospital or owner of the approved place shall send to the Chief Medical Officer of the Sate, IN form II a monthly statement of cases where medical termination of pregnancy has been done.

(6) On every envelope referred to in sub-regulation (1), pertaining to the termination of pregnancy under section 5, there shall be noted the name and address of the registered medical practitioner by whom the pregnancy was terminated and the date on which the pregnancy was terminated and such envelope shall be marked "SECRET".

Explanation. The columns pertaining to the hospital or approved place and the serial number assigned to the pregnant woman in the Admission Register shall be left blank in Form I in the case of termination performed under section 5.

(7) Where the pregnancy is not terminated in an approved place or hospital, every envelope referred to in sub-regulation (6) shall be sent by registered post to the Chief Medical Officer of the State on the same day on which the pregnancy was terminated or on the working day next following the day on which the pregnancy was terminated:

Provided that where the pregnancy is terminated in an approved place or hospital, the procedure provided in sub-regulations (1) to (6) shall be followed.

5. Maintenance of Admission Register:

(1) Every head of the hospital or owner of the approved place shall maintain a register in form III for recording there in the details of the admissions of women for the termination of their pregnancies and keep such register for a period of five years from the end of the calendar year it relates to.

(2) The entries in the Admission Register shall be made serially and a fresh serial shall be started at the commencement of each calendar year and the serial number of the particular year shall be distinguished from the serial number of other years by mentioning the year against the serial number, for example, serial number 5 of 1972 and serial number 5 of 1973 shall be mentioned as 5/1972 and 5/1973.

(3) Admission Register shall be a secret document and the information contained therein as to the name and other particulars of the pregnant woman shall not be disclosed to any person.

6. Admission Register not to be open to inspection:

The Admission Register shall be kept in the safe custody of the head of the hospital or owner of the approved place, or by any person authorized by such head or owner and save as otherwise provided in sub-regulation (5) of regulation 4 shall not be open for inspection by any person except under the authority of law:

Provided that the registered medical practitioner on the application of an employed woman whose pregnancy has been terminated, grant a certificate for the purpose of enabling her to obtain leave from her employer;

Provided further that any such employer shall not disclose this information to any other person.

7. Entries in registers maintained in hospital or approved place:

No entry shall be made in any case-sheet, operation theatre register, follow-up card or any other document or register other than the admission Register maintained at any hospital or approved place indicating therein the name of the pregnant woman and reference to the pregnant woman shall be made therein by the serial number assigned to the woman in the Admission Register.

Form I
(See Regulation 3)

I____

(Name and qualifications of the Registered Medical Practitioner in block letters)

____

(Full address of the Registered Medical Practitioner)

____

(Name and qualifications of the Registered Medical Practitioner in block letters)

____

(Full address of the Registered Medical Practitioner) hereby certify that *I/We am/are of opinion, formed in good faith, that it is necessary to terminate the pregnancy of

____

(Full name of pregnant women in block letters) resident of

____

(Full address of pregnant women in block letters)

for the reasons given below**.

* I/We hereby give intimation that *I/We terminated the pregnancy of the woman referred to above who bears the serial no. ________________ in the Admission Register of the hospital/ approved place.

Place: Signature of the Registered Medical Practitioner

Date: Signature of the Registered Medical Practitioners

*Strike out whichever is not applicable,
** of the reasons specified items (i) to (v) write the one which is appropriate.

(i) in order to save the life of the pregnant women,
(ii) in order to prevent grave injury to the physical and mental health of the pregnant women,
(iii) in view of the substantial risk that if the child was born it would suffer from such physical or mental abnormalities as to be seriously handicapped,
(iv) as the pregnancy is alleged by pregnant women to have been caused by rape,
(v) as the pregnancy has occurred as result of failure of any contraceptive device or methods used by married woman or her husband for the purpose of limiting the number of children.

Note: Account may be taken of the pregnant women's actual or reasonably foreseeable environment in determining whether the continuance of her pregnancy would involve a grave injury to her physical or mental health.

Place: Signature of the Registered Medical Practitioner

Date: Signature of the Registered Medical Practitioners

Form II
[See Regulation 4(5)]

1. Name of the State
2. Name of the hospital/approved place
3. Duration of pregnancy (give total No. only)
   (a) Up to 12 weeks.
   (b) Between 12–20 weeks
4. Religion of woman
   (a) Hindu
   (b) Muslim
   (c) Christian
   (d) Others
   (e) Total
5. Termination with acceptance of contraception:
   (a) Sterilisation
   (b) I.U.D.
6. Reasons for termination:
   (give total number under each sub-head)
   (a) Danger to life of the pregnant woman.
   (b) Grave injury to the physical health of the pregnant woman.
   (c) Grave injury to the mental health of the pregnant woman.
   (d) Pregnancy caused by rape.
   (e) Substantial risk that if the child was born, it would suffer from such physical or mental abnormalities as to be seriously handicapped.
   (f) Failure of any contraceptive device or method.

Signature of the Officer Incharge with Date

Form III
(See Regulation 5)
Admission Register

(To be destroyed on the expiry of five years from the dated of the last entry in the register)

1	2	3	4	5	6	7
S. No.	*Date of Admission*	*Name of the Patient*	*Wife/Daughter of*	*Age*	*Religion*	*Address*

8	9	10	11	12	13	14
Duration of Pregnancy	*Reasons on which Pregnancy is terminated*	*Date of termination of Pregnancy*	*Date of discharge of patient*	*Result and Remarks*	*Name of Registered Medical Practitioner (s) by who the opinion is formed*	*Name of Registered Medical Practitioner (s) by whom Pregnancy is terminated*

Appendix III
Medical Termination of Pregnancy Rules, 2003

In exercise of powers conferred by section 6 of the Medical Termination of Pregnancy Act, 1971 (34 of 1971), the Central Government hereby makes the following rules, namely:

1. Short title and commencement:
   (1) These rules may be called the Medical Termination of Pregnancy Rules, 2003.
   (2) They shall come into force on the date of their publication in the Official Gazette.
2. Definitions:
   In this rules, unless the context otherwise requires,
   (a) "Act" means the Medical Termination of Pregnancy Act, 1971 (34 of 1971);
   (b) "Chief Medical Officer" means the Chief Medical Officer of a district, by whatever name called;
   (c) "Form" means a form appended to these rules;
   (d) "owner" in relation to a place means any person who is the administrative head or otherwise responsible for the working or maintenance of a hospital or place, by whatever name called, where the pregnancy may be terminated under this Act;
   (e) "Committee" means a committee constituted at the district level under the proviso to clause (b) of section 4 read with Rule 3.
3. Composition and tenure of District Level Committee:
   (1) One member of the district level Committee shall be the Gynaecologist/Surgeon/Anaesthetist and other members from the local medical profession, non-governmental organizations, and Panchayati Raj Institution of the district.
   Provided that one of the members of the Committee shall be a woman.
   (2) Tenure of the committee shall be for two calendar years and the tenure of the non-Government members shall not be more than two terms.

4. Experience and training under clause (d) of section 2.

For the purpose of clause (d) of section (2), a registered medical practitioner shall have one or more of the following experience or training in gynaecology and obstetrics, namely:

(a) In the case of a medical practitioner, who was registered in a State Medical Register immediately before the commencement of the Act, experience in the practice of gynaecology and obstetrics for a period of not less than three years;

(b) In the case of a medical practitioner, who is registered in a State Medical Register:

  (i) if he has completed six months of house surgency in gynaecology and obstetrics; or

  (ii) unless the following facilities are provided therein, if he had experience at any hospital for a period of not less than one year in the practice of obstetrics and gynaecology; or

(c) If he has assisted a registered medical practitioner in the performance of twenty-five cases of medical termination of pregnancy of which at least five have been performed independently, in a hospital established or maintained, or a training institute approved for this purpose by the Government.

  (i) This training would enable the Registered Medical Practitioner (RMP) to do only 1st Trimester terminations (up to 12 weeks of gestation).

  (ii) For terminations up to twenty weeks the experience or training as prescribed under sub-rules (a), (b) and (d) shall apply.

(d) In case of a medical practitioner who has been registered in a State Medical Register and who holds a port-graduate degree or diploma in gynaecology and obstetrics, the experience or training gained during the course of such degree or diploma.

5. Approval of a place:

(1) No place shall be approved under clause (b) of section 4.

(i) Unless the Government is satisfied that termination of pregnancies may be done therein under safe and hygienic conditions; and

(ii) Unless the following facilities are provided therein, namely:

in case of first trimester, that is, up to 12 weeks of pregnancy:

a gynecology examination/labour table, resuscitation and sterilization equipment, drugs and parental fluid, back up facilities for treatment of shock and facilities for transportation; and in case of second trimester, that is up to 20 weeks of pregnancy:

(a) an operation table and instruments for performing abdominal or gynaecological surgery;

(b) anaesthetic equipment, resuscitation equipment and sterilization equipment;

(c) drugs and parental fluids for emergency use, notified by Government of India from time to time.

Explanation. In the case of termination of early pregnancy up to seven weeks using RU-486 with Misoprostol, the same may be prescribed by a Registered Medical Practitioner (RMP) as defined under clause (d) of section 2 of the Act and section 4 of MTP Rules, at his clinic, provided such a Registered Medical Practitioner has access to a place approved under section 4 of the MTP Act, 1971 read with MTP Amendment Act, 2002 and Rules 5 of the MTP Rules. For the purpose of access, the RMP should display a Certificate to this effect from the owner of the approved place.

(2) Every application for the approval of a place shall be in a Form A and shall be addressed to the Chief Medical Officer of the district.

(3) On receipt of an application under sub-rule (2), the Chief Medical Officer of the district may verify any information contained, in any such application or inspect any such place with a view to satisfying himself that the facilities referred to in sub-rule (1) are provided, and that termination of pregnancies may be made under safe and hygienic conditions.

(4) Every owner of the place which is inspected by the Chief Medical Officer of the district shall afford all reasonable facilities for the inspection of the place.

(5) The Chief Medical Officer of the district may, if he is satisfied after such verification, enquiry or inspection, as may be considered necessary, that termination of pregnancies may be done under safe and hygienic conditions, at the place, recommend the approval of such place to the Committee.

(6) The Committee may after considering the application and the recommendations of the Chief Medical Officer of the district approve such place and issue a certificate of approval in Form B.

(7) The certificate of approval issued by the Committee shall be conspicuously displaced at the place to be easily visible to persons visiting the place.

(8) The place shall be inspected within two months of receiving the application and certificate of approval may be issued within the next two months, or in case any deficiency has been noted, within two months of the deficiency having been rectified by the applicant.

(9) On the commencement of these rules, a place approved in accordance with the Medical Termination of Pregnancy Rules, 1975 shall be deemed to have been approved under these rules.

6. Inspection of a place:

(1) A place approved under Rule 5 may be inspected by the Chief Medical Officer of the district, as often as may be necessary with a view to verify whether termination of pregnancies is being done therein under safe and, hygienic conditions.

(2) If the Chief Medical Officer has reason to believe that there has been death of, or injury to, a pregnant woman at the place or that termination of pregnancies is not being done at the place under safe and hygienic conditions, he may call for any information or may seize any article, medicine, ampoule, admission register or other document, maintained, kept or found at the place.

(3) The provisions of the Code of Criminal Procedure, 1973 (2 of 1974), relating to seizure, so far as it may, apply to seizure made under sub-rule (2).

7. Cancellation or suspension of certificate of approval:

(1) If, after inspection of any place approved under Rule 5, the Chief medical Officer of the district is satisfied that the facilities specified in Rule 5 are not being properly maintained therein and the termination of pregnancy at such place cannot be made under safe and hygienic conditions, he shall make a report of the fact to the Committee giving the detail of the deficiencies or defects found at the place and the committee may, if it is satisfied, suspend or cancel the approval provided that the committee shall give an opportunity of making representation to the owner of the place before the certificate issued under Rule 5 is cancelled.

(2) Where a certificate issued under Rule 5 is cancelled, the owner of the place may make such additions or improvements in the place and there after, he may make an application to the Committee for grant of approval under Rule 5.

(3) In the event of suspension of a certificate, of approval, the place shall not be deemed to be an approved place during the suspension for the purposes of termination of pregnancy from the date of communication of the order of such suspension.

8. Review:

(1) The owner of a place, who is aggrieved by an order made under Rule 7, may make an application for

review of the order to the Government within a period of sixty days from the date of such order:

Provided that the Government may condone any delay in case it is satisfied that applicant was prevented by sufficient cause to make application within time.

(2) The Government may, after giving the owner an opportunity of being heard, confirm, modify or reverse the order.

9. Form of consent:

The consent referred to in sub-section (4) of section 3 shall be given in Form C.

10. Repeal and saving:

The Medical Termination of Pregnancy Rules, 1975, are hereby repealed except as respects things done or omitted to be done before such repeal.

Form A
(See sub-rule (2) of Rule 5)

Form of application for the approval of a place under clause (b) of section 4

Category of approved place:

A. Pregnancy can be terminated upto 12 weeks

B. Pregnancy can be terminated upto 20 weeks

1. Name of the place (in capital letters)
2. Address in full
3. Non-government/Private/Nursing/Home/Other Institutions
4. State, if the following facilities are available at the place

Category A

(i) Gynecological examination/labour table.
(ii) Resuscitation equipment.
(iii) Sterilization equipment.
(iv) Facilities for treatment of shock, including emergency drugs.
(v) Facilities for transportation, if required.

Category B

(ii) An operation table and Instruments for performing abdominal or gynaecological surgery.
(iii) Drugs and parental fluid in sufficient supply for emergency cases.
(iv) Anaesthetic equipment, resuscitation equipment and sterilization equipment.

Place :

Date :

Signature of the Owner of the Place

Form B
(See sub-rule (6) of Rule 5)
Certificate of Approval

The place described below is hereby approved for the purpose of the Medical Termination of Pregnancy Act, 1971 (34 of 1971).

As read within upto________________________weeks

Name of the place

Address and other descriptions

Name of the owner

Place :

Date :

To the Government of the_________________________

Form C
(See Rule 9)

I________________daughter/wife____________aged about ________________ years of__________at present residing at (here state the permanent address)

____

____

do hereby give my consent to the termination of my pregnancy at ______________________________(State the name of place where the pregnancy is to be terminated)

Place:
Date:

Signature

(To be filled in by guardian where the woman is a mentally ill person or minor)

I____

son/daughter/wife of______________________________aged about years of____at present residing at (Permanent address) ________________

____do hereby give my consent to the termination of the pregnancy of my ward __________________________________who is a minor/lunatic at______________________________place of termination of my pregnancy)

Place:
Date:

Form II
[See Regulation 4(5)]

1. Name of the state
2. Name of the hospital/approved place
3. Duration of pregnancy (give total No. only)
   (a) Up to 12 weeks
   (b) Between 12–20 weeks
4. Religion of woman
   (a) Hindu
   (b) Muslim
   (c) Christian
   (d) Others
   (e) Total
5. Termination with acceptance of contraception:
   (a) Sterilisation
   (b) I.U.D.
6. Reasons for termination:
   (give total number under each sub-head)
   (a) Danger to life of the pregnant woman.
   (b) Grave injury to the physical health of the pregnant woman.
   (c) Grave injury to the mental health of the pregnant woman.
   (d) Pregnancy caused by rape.
   (e) Substantial risk that if the child was born, it would suffer from such physical or mental abnormalities as to be seriously handicapped.
   (f) Failure of any contraceptive device or method.

Signature of the Officer Incharge with Date

Form III
(See Regulation 5)
Admission Register

(To be destroyed on the expiry of five years from the dated of the last entry in the Register)

1	2	3	4	5	6	7
S. No.	*Date of Admission*	*Name of the Patient*	*Wife/Daughter of*	*Age*	*Religion*	*Address*

8	9	10	11	12	13	14
Duration of Pregnancy	*Reasons on which Pregnancy is terminated*	*Date of termination of Pregnancy*	*Date of discharge of patient*	*Result and Remarks*	*Name of Registered Medical Practitioner (s) by who the opinion is formed*	*Name of Registered Medical Practitioner (s) by whom Pregnancy is terminated*

Appendix IV
The Pre-Natal Diagnostic Techniques (Regulation and Prevention of Misuse) Act, 1994 (Act No. 57 of 1994) and The Pre-Natal Diagnostic Techniques (Regulation and Prevention of Misuse) Amendment Act, 2002 (No.14 of 2003)

[20th September, 1994]

An Act to provide *for the prohibition of sex selection, before or after conception, and* for regulation of prenatal diagnostic techniques for the purposes of detecting genetic abnormalities or metabolic disorders or chromosomal abnormalities or certain congenital malformations or sex-linked disorders and for the prevention of their misuse for sex determination leading to female foeticide; and, for matters connected therewith or incidental thereto.

BE it enacted by Parliament in the Forty-fifth Year of the Republic of India as follows:

Chapter I
Preliminary

1. Short title, extent and commencement: (1) This Act may be called the Pre-conception and Prenatal Diagnostic Techniques (Prohibition of Sex Selection) Act, 1994. (2) It shall extend to the whole of India except the State of Jammu and Kashmir. (3) It shall come into force on such date as the Central Government may, by notification in the Official Gazette, appoint.
2. Definitions: In this Act, unless the context otherwise requires:
   (a) "Appropriate Authority" means the Appropriate Authority appointed under section 17;
   (b) "Board" means the Central Supervisory Board constituted under section 7;

(ba) "conceptus" means any product of conception at any stage of development from fertilization until birth including extra embryonic membranes as well as the embryo or foetus;

(bb) "embryo" means a developing human organism after fertilization till the end of eight weeks (fifty-six days);

(bc) "foetus" means a human organism during the period of its development beginning on the fifty-seventh day following fertilization or creation (excluding any time in which its development has been suspended) and ending at the birth;

(c) "Genetic Counseling Centre" means an institute, hospital, nursing home or any place, by whatever name called, which provides for genetic counselling to patients;

(d) "Genetic Clinic" means a clinic, institute, hospital, nursing home or any place, by whatever name called, which is used for conducting pre-natal diagnostic procedures.

Explanation: For the purposes of this clause, 'Genetic Clinic' includes a vehicle, where ultrasound machine or imaging machine or scanner or other equipment capable of determining sex of the foetus or a portable equipment which has the potential for detection of sex during pregnancy or selection of sex before conception, is used.

(e) "Genetic Laboratory" means a laboratory and includes a place where facilities are provided for conducting analysis or tests of samples received from Genetic Clinic for pre-natal diagnostic test.

Explanation: For the purposes of this clause, 'Genetic Laboratory' includes a place where ultra-sound machine or imaging machine or scanner or other equipment capable of determining sex of the foetus or a portable equipment which has the potential for detection of sex during pregnancy or selection of sex before conception, is used.

(f) "Gynaecologist" means a person who possesses a post-graduate qualification in gynaecology and obstetrics;

(g) "Medical geneticist" includes a person who possesses a degree or diploma in genetic science in the fields of sex selection and pre-natal diagnostic techniques or has experience of not less than two years in such field after obtaining:

  (i) any one of the medical qualifications recognised under the Indian Medical Council Act, 1956 (102 of 1956); or

  (ii) a post-graduate degree in biological sciences;

(h) "Pediatrician" means a person who possesses a post-graduate qualification in pediatrics;

(i) "pre-natal diagnostic procedures" means all gynaecological or obstetrical or medical procedures such as ultrasonography, foetoscopy, taking or removing samples of amniotic fluid, chorionic villi, blood or any other tissue or fluid of a man, or of a woman for being sent to a Genetic Laboratory or Genetic Clinic for conducting any type of analysis or pre-natal diagnostic tests for selection of sex before or after conception;

(j) "pre-natal diagnostic techniques" includes all pre-natal diagnostic procedures and pre-natal diagnostic tests;

(k) "pre-natal diagnostic test" means ultrasonography or any test or analysis of amniotic fluid, chorionic villi, blood or any tissue or fluid of a pregnant woman or conceptus conducted to detect genetic or metabolic disorders or chromosomal abnormalities or congenital anomalies or haemoglobinopathies or sex-linked diseases;

(l) "prescribed" means prescribed by rules made under this Act;

(m) "registered medical practitioner" means a medical practitioner who possesses any recognised medical qualification as defined in clause (h) of section 2 of the Indian Medical Council Act, 1956 (102 of 1956) and whose name has been entered in a State Medical Register;

(n) "regulations" means regulations framed by the Board under this Act;

(o) "sex selection" includes any procedure, technique, test or administration or prescription or provision of anything for the purpose of ensuring or increasing the probability that an embryo will be of a particular sex;

(p) "sonologist or imaging specialist" means a person who possesses any one of the medical qualifications recognized under the Indian Medical Council Act, 1956 or who possesses a postgraduate qualification in ultrasonography or imaging techniques or radiology;

(q) "State Board" means a State Supervisory Board or a Union territory Supervisory Board constituted under Section 16A;

(r) "State Government" in relation to Union territory with Legislature means the Administrator of that Union territory appointed by the President under Article 239 of Constitution.

Chapter II
Regulation of Genetic Counselling Centres, Genetic Laboratories and Genetic Clinics

3. Regulation of Genetic Counselling Centres, Genetic Laboratories and Genetic Clinics on and from the commencement of this Act:

   1. no Genetic Counselling Centre, Genetic Laboratory or Genetic Clinic unless registered under this Act, shall conduct or associate with, or help in, conducting activities relating to prenatal diagnostic techniques;
   2. no Genetic Counselling Centre or Genetic Laboratory or Genetic Clinic shall employ or cause to be employed or take services of any person, whether on honorary basis or on payment who does not possess qualifications as may be prescribed;

3. no medical geneticist, gynaecologist, paediatrician, registered medical practitioner or any other person shall conduct or cause to be conducted or aid in conducting by himself or through any other person, any pre-natal diagnostic techniques at a place other than a place registered under this Act.

3A. Prohibition of sex-selection: No person, including a specialist or a team of specialists in the field of infertility, shall conduct or cause to be conducted or aid in conducting by himself or by any other person, sex selection on a woman or a man or on both or on any tissue, embryo, conceptus, fluid or gametes derived from either or both of them.

3B. Prohibition on sale of ultrasound machines, etc., to persons, laboratories, clinics, etc. not registered under the Act- No person shall sell any ultrasound machine or imaging machine or scanner or any other equipment capable of detecting sex of foetus to any Genetic Counselling Centre, Genetic Laboratory, Genetic Clinic or any other person not registered under the Act.

Chapter III
Regulation of Pre-Natal Diagnostic Techniques

4. Regulation of pre-natal diagnostic techniques on and from the commencement of this Act:
   1. no place including a registered Genetic Counselling Centre or Genetic Laboratory or Genetic Clinic shall be used or caused to be used by any person for conducting pre-natal diagnostic techniques except for the purposes specified in clause (2) and after satisfying any of the conditions specified in clause (3);
   2. no pre-natal diagnostic techniques shall be conducted except for the purposes of detection of any of the following abnormalities, namely:
      (i) chromosomal abnormalities;
      (ii) genetic metabolic diseases;
      (iii) haemoglobinopathies;

(iv) sex-linked genetic diseases;
(v) congenital anomalies; and
(vi) any other abnormalities or diseases as may be specified by the Central Supervisory Board.

3. no pre-natal diagnostic techniques shall be used or conducted unless the person qualified to do so is satisfied for reasons to be recorded in writing that any of the following conditions are fulfilled, namely:
(i) age of the pregnant woman is above thirty-five years;
(ii) the pregnant woman has undergone of two or more spontaneous abortions or foetal loss;
(iii) the pregnant woman had been exposed to potentially teratogenic agents such as drugs, radiation, infection or chemicals;
(iv) the pregnant woman or her spouse has a family history of mental retardation or physical deformities such as, spasticity or any other genetic disease;
(v) any other condition as may be specified by the Central Supervisory Board;

Provided that the person conducting ultrasonography on a pregnant woman shall keep complete record thereof in the clinic in such manner, as may be prescribed, and any deficiency or inaccuracy found therein shall amount to contravention of provisions of section 5 or section 6 unless contrary is proved by the person conducting such ultrasonography;

4. no person including a relative or husband of the pregnant woman shall seek or encourage the conduct of any pre-natal diagnostic techniques on her except for the purposes specified in clause (2).
5. no person including a relative or husband of a woman shall seek or encourage the conduct of any sex-selection technique on her or him or both.

5. Written consent of pregnant woman and prohibition of communicating the sex of foetus.

1. No person referred to in clause (2) of section 3 shall conduct the pre-natal diagnostic procedures unless:

(a) he has explained all known side and after effects of such procedures to the pregnant woman concerned;

(b) he has obtained in the prescribed form her written consent to undergo such procedures in the language which she understands; and

(c) a copy of her written consent obtained under clause (b) is given to the pregnant woman.

2. No person including the person conducting pre-natal diagnostic procedures shall communicate to the pregnant woman concerned or her relatives or any other person the sex of the foetus by words, signs or in any other manner.

6. Determination of sex prohibited on and from the commencement of this Act:

(a) no Genetic Counselling Centre or Genetic Laboratory or Genetic Clinic shall conduct or cause to be conducted in its Centre, Laboratory or Clinic, pre-natal diagnostic techniques including ultrasonography, for the purpose of determining the sex of a foetus;

(b) no person shall conduct or cause to be conducted any pre-natal diagnostic techniques including ultrasonography for the purpose of determining the sex of a foetus;

(c) no person shall, by whatever means, cause or allow to be caused selection of sex before or after conception.

Chapter IV
Central Supervisory Board

7. Constitution of Central Supervisory Board:

1. The Central Government shall constitute a Board to be known as the Central Supervisory Board to exercise the powers and perform the functions conferred on the Board under this Act.

2. The Board shall consist of:

(a) the Minister in charge of the Ministry or Department of Family Welfare, who shall be the Chairman, ex-officio;

(b) the Secretary to the Government of India in charge of the Department of Family Welfare, who shall be the Vice-Chairman, ex-officio;

(c) three members to be appointed by the Central Government to represent the Ministries of Central Government in charge of Women and Child Development, Department of Legal Affairs or Legislative Department in the Ministry of Law and Justice, and Indian System of Medicine and Homoeopathy, ex-officio;

(d) the Director General of Health Services of the Central Government, ex-officio;

(e) ten members to be appointed by the Central Government, two each from amongst
   (i) eminent medical geneticists;
   (ii) eminent gynaecologist and obstetrician or expert of stri-roga or prasuti-tantra;
   (iii) eminent paediatricians;
   (iv) eminent social scientists; and
   (v) representatives of women welfare organisations;

(f) three women Members of Parliament, of whom two shall be elected by the House of the People and one by the Council of States;

(g) four members to be appointed by the Central Government by rotation to represent the States and the Union territories, two in the alphabetical order and two in the reverse alphabetical order:
Provided that no appointment under this clause shall be made except on the recommendation of the State Government or, as the case may be, the Union territory;

(h) an officer, not below the rank of a Joint Secretary or equivalent of the Central Government, in charge of Family Welfare, who shall be the Member-Secretary, ex-officio.

8. Terms of office of members:
   (1) The term of office of a member, other than an ex-officio member, shall be
      (a) in case of appointment under clause (e) or clause (f) of sub-section (2) of section 7, three years; and
      (b) in case of appointment under clause (g) of the said subsection, one year.
   2. If a casual vacancy occurs in the office of any other members, whether by reason of his death, resignation or inability to discharge his functions owing to illness or other incapacity, such vacancy shall be filled by the Central Government by making a fresh appointment and the member so appointed shall hold office for the remainder of the term of office of the person in whose place he is so appointed.
   3. The Vice-Chairman shall perform such functions as may be assigned to him by the Chairman from time to time.
   4. The procedure to be followed by the members in the discharge of their functions shall be such as may be prescribed.
9. Meetings of the Board:
   1. The Board shall meet at such time and place, and shall observe such rules of procedure in regard to the transaction of business at its meetings (including the quorum at such meetings) as may be provided by regulations:

      Provided that the Board shall meet at least once in six months.
   2. The Chairman and in his absence the Vice-Chairman shall preside at the meetings of the Board.
   3. If for any reason the Chairman or the Vice-Chairman is unable to attend any meeting of the Board, any other member chosen by the members present at the meeting shall preside at the meeting.
   4. All questions which come up before any meeting of the Board shall be decided by a majority of the votes

of the members present and voting, and in the event of an equality of votes, the Chairman, or in his absence, the person presiding, shall have and exercise a second or casting vote.

5. Members other than ex-officio members shall receive such allowances, if any, from the Board as may be prescribed.

10. Vacancies, etc., not to invalidate proceedings of the Board: No act or proceeding of the Board shall be invalid merely by reason of

   (a) any vacancy in, or any defect in the constitution of, the Board; or
   (b) any defect in the appointment of a person acting as a member of the Board; or
   (c) any irregularity in the procedure of the Board not affecting the merits of the case.

11. Temporary association of persons with the Board for particular purposes:

   1. The Board may associate with itself, in such manner and for such purposes as may be determined by regulations, any person whose assistance or advice it may desire in carrying out any of the provisions of this Act.
   2. A person associated with it by the Board under sub-section (1) for any purpose shall have a right to take part in the discussions relevant to that purpose, but shall not have a right to vote at a meeting of the Board and shall not be a member for any other purpose.

12. Appointment or officers and other employees of the Board:

   1. For the purpose of enabling it efficiently to discharge its functions under this Act, the Board may, subject to such regulations as may be made in this behalf, appoint (whether on deputation or otherwise) such number of officers and other employees as it may consider necessary:

      Provided that the appointment of such category of officers, as may be specified in such regulations, shall be subject to the approval of the Central Government.

2. Every officer or other employee appointed by the Board shall be subject to such conditions of service and shall be entitled to such remuneration as may be specified in the regulations.

13. Authentication of orders and other instruments of the Board: All orders and decisions of the Board shall be authenticated by the signature of the Chairman or any other member authorised by the Board in this behalf, and all other instruments issued by the Board shall be authenticated by the signature of the Member-Secretary or any other officer of the Board authorised in like manner in this behalf.

14. Disqualifications for appointment as member: A person shall be disqualified for being appointed as a member if, he
    (a) has been convicted and sentenced to imprisonment for an offence which, in the opinion of the Central Government, involves moral turpitude; or
    (b) is an undischarged insolvent; or
    (c) is of unsound mind and stands so declared by a competent court; or
    (d) has been removed or dismissed from the service of the Government or a Corporation owned or controlled by the Government; or
    (e) has, in the opinion of the Central Government, such financial or other interest in the Board as is likely to affect prejudicially the discharge by him of his functions as a member; or
    (f) has, in the opinion of the Central Government, been associated with the use or promotion of pre-natal diagnostic technique for determination of sex or with any sex selection technique.

15. Eligibility of member for reappointment: Subject to the other terms and conditions of service as may be prescribed, any person ceasing to be a member shall be eligible for reappointment as such member.

    Provided that no member other than an ex-officio member shall be appointed for more than two consecutive terms.

16. Functions of the Board: The Board shall have the following functions, namely:
    (i) to advise the Central Government on policy matters relating to use of pre-natal diagnostic techniques, sex selection techniques and against their misuse;
    (ii) to review and monitor implementation of the Act and rules made thereunder and recommend to the Central Government changes in the said Act and rules;
    (iii) to create public awareness against the practice of pre-conception sex selection and prenatal determination of sex of foetus leading to female foeticide;
    (iv) to lay down code of conduct to be observed by persons working at Genetic Counselling Centres, Genetic Laboratories and Genetic Clinics;
    (v) to oversee the performance of various bodies constituted under the Act and take appropriate steps to ensure its proper and effective implementation;
    (vi) any other functions as may be prescribed under the Act.

16A. Constitution of State Supervisory Board and Union territory Supervisory Board:
    1. Each State and Union territory having Legislature shall constitute a Board to be known as the State Supervisory Board or the Union territory Supervisory Board, as the case may be, which shall have the following functions:
        (i) to create public awareness against the practice of pre-conception sex selection and pre-natal determination of sex of foetus leading to female foeticide in the State;
        (ii) to review the activities of the Appropriate Authorities functioning in the State and recommend appropriate action against them;
        (iii) to monitor the implementation of provisions of the Act and the rules and make suitable recommendations relating thereto, to the Board;

- (iv) to send such consolidated reports as may be prescribed in respect of the various activities undertaken in the State under the Act to the Board and the Central Government; and
- (v) any other functions as may be prescribed under the Act.

2. The State Board shall consist of
   - (a) the Minister in charge of Health and Family Welfare in the State, who shall be the Chairperson, ex-officio;
   - (b) the Secretary in charge of the Department of Health and Family Welfare who shall be the Vice-Chairperson, ex-officio;
   - (c) Secretaries or Commissioners in charge of Departments of Women and Child Development, Social Welfare, Law and Indian System of Medicines and Homoeopathy, ex-officio, or their representatives;
   - (d) Director of Health and Family Welfare or Indian System of Medicines and Homoeopathy of the State Government, ex-officio;
   - (e) Three women members of Legislative Assembly or Legislative Council;
   - (f) Ten members to be appointed by the State Government out of which two each shall be from the following categories:
     - (i) eminent social scientists and legal experts;
     - (ii) eminent women activists from non-governmental organizations or otherwise;
     - (iii) eminent gynaecologists and obstetricians or experts of stri-roga or prasuti tantra;
     - (iv) eminent paediatricians or medical geneticists;
     - (v) eminent radiologists or sonologists;
   - (g) an officer not below the rank of Joint Director in charge of Family Welfare, who shall be the Member Secretary, ex-officio.
3. The State Board shall meet at least once in four months.

4. The term of office of a member, other than an ex-officio member, shall be three years.
5. If a vacancy occurs in the office of any member other than an ex-officio member, it shall be filled by making fresh appointment.
6. If a member of the Legislative Assembly or member of the Legislative Council who is a member of the State Board, becomes Minister or Speaker or Deputy Speaker of the Legislative Assembly or Chairperson or Deputy Chairperson of the Legislative Council, she shall cease to be a member of the State Board.
7. One-third of the total number of members of the State Board shall constitute the quorum.
8. The State Board may co-opt a member as and when required, provided that the number of coopted members does not exceed one-third of the total strength of the State Board.
9. The co-opted members shall have the same powers and functions as other members, except the right to vote and shall abide by the rules and regulations.
10. In respect of matters not specified in this section, the State Board shall follow procedures and conditions as are applicable to the Board.

Chapter V
Appropriate Authority and Advisory Committee

17. Appropriate Authority and Advisory Committee:
    1. The Central Government shall appoint, by notification in the Official Gazette, one or more Appropriate Authorities for each of the Union territories for the purposes of this Act.
    2. The State Government shall appoint, by notification in the Official Gazette, one or more Appropriate Authorities for the whole or part of the State for the purposes of this Act having regard to the intensity of the problem of pre-natal sex determination leading to female foeticide.

3. The officers appointed as Appropriate Authorities under sub-section (1) or sub-section (2) shall be:

    (a) when appointed for the whole of the State or the Union territory, consisting of the following three members

        (i) an officer of or above the rank of the Joint Director of Health and Family Welfare-Chairperson;

        (ii) an eminent woman representing women's organization; and

        (iii) an officer of Law Department of the State or the Union territory concerned:

        Provided that it shall be the duty of the State or the Union territory concerned to constitute multimember State or Union territory level Appropriate Authority within three months of the coming into force of the Pre-natal Diagnostic Techniques (Regulation and Prevention of Misuse) Amendment Act, 2002:

        Provided further that any vacancy occurring therein shall be filled within three months of that occurrence.

    (b) when appointed for any part of the State or the Union territory, of such other rank as the State Government or the Central Government, as the case may be, may deem fit.

4. The Appropriate Authority shall have the following functions, namely:

    (a) to grant, suspend or cancel registration of a Genetic Counselling Centre, Genetic Laboratory or Genetic Clinic;

    (b) to enforce standards prescribed for the Genetic Counselling Centre, Genetic Laboratory and Genetic Clinic;

(c) to investigate complaints of breach of the provisions of this Act or the rules made thereunder and take immediate action;

(d) to seek and consider the advice of the Advisory Committee, constituted under sub-section (5) on application for registration and on complaints for suspension or cancellation of registration;

(e) to take appropriate legal action against the use of any sex selection technique by any person at any place, suo motu or brought to its notice and also to initiate independent investigations in such matter;

(f) to create public awareness against the practice of sex selection or pre-natal determination of sex;

(g) to supervise the implementation of the provisions of the Act and rules;

(h) to recommend to the CSB and State Boards modifications required in the rules in accordance with changes in technology or social conditions;

(i) to take action on the recommendations of the Advisory Committee made after investigation of complaint for suspension or cancellation of registration.

5. The Central Government or the State Government, as the case may be, shall constitute an Advisory Committee for each Appropriate Authority to aid and advise the Appropriate Authority in the discharge of its functions, and shall appoint one of the members of the Advisory Committee to be its Chairman.

6. The Advisory Committee shall consist of:

(a) three medical experts from amongst gynaecologists, obstetricans, paediatricians and medical geneticists;

(b) one legal expert;

(c) one officer to represent the department dealing with information and publicity of the State Government or the Union territory, as the case may be;

(d) three eminent social workers of whom not less than one shall be from amongst representatives of women's organisations.

7. No person who has been associated with the use or promotion of pre-natal diagnostic technique for determination of sex or sex selection shall be appointed as a member of the Advisory Committee.

8. The Advisory Committee may meet as and when it thinks fit or on the request of the Appropriate Authority for consideration of any application for registration or any complaint for suspension or cancellation of registration and to give advice thereon:

Provided that the period intervening between any two meetings shall not exceed the prescribed period.

9. The terms and conditions subject to which a person may be appointed to the Advisory Committee and the procedure to be followed by such Committee in the discharge of its functions shall be such as may be prescribed.

17A. Powers of Appropriate Authorities: The Appropriate Authority shall have the powers in respect of the following matters, namely:

(a) summoning of any person who is in possession of any information relating to violation of the provisions of this Act or the rules made thereunder;

(b) production of any document or material object relating to clause (a);

(c) issuing search warrant for any place suspected to be indulging in sex selection techniques or pre-natal sex determination; and

(d) any other matter which may be prescribed.

Chapter VI
Registration of Genetic Counselling Centres Genetic Laboratories and Genetic Clinics

18. Registration of Genetic Counselling Centres, Genetic Laboratories or Genetic Clinics:

    (1) No person shall open any Genetic Counselling Centre, Genetic Laboratory or Genetic Clinic, including clinic, laboratory or centre having ultra-sound or imaging machine or scanner or any other technology capable of undertaking determination of sex of foetus and sex selection, or render services to any of them, after the commencement of the Pre-natal Diagnostic Techniques (Regulation and Prevention of Misuse) Amendment Act, 2002 unless such centre, laboratory or clinic is duly registered under the Act.

    2. Every application for registration under sub-section (1), shall be made to the Appropriate Authority in such form and in such manner and shall be accompanied by such fees as may be prescribed.

    3. Every Genetic Counselling Centre, Genetic Laboratory or Genetic Clinic engaged, either partly or exclusively, in counselling or conducting pre-natal diagnostic techniques for any of the purposes mentioned in section 4, immediately before the commencement of this Act, shall apply for registration within sixty days from the date of such commencement.

    4. Subject to the provisions of section 6, every Genetic Counselling Centre, Genetic Laboratory or Genetic Clinic engaged in counselling or conducting pre-natal diagnostic techniques shall cease to conduct any such counselling or technique on the expiry of six months from the date of commencement of this Act unless such Centre, Laboratory or Clinic has applied for registration and is so registered separately or jointly or till such application is disposed of, whichever is earlier.

5. No Genetic Counselling Centre, Genetic Laboratory or Genetic Clinic shall be registered under this Act unless the Appropriate Authority is satisfied that such Centre, Laboratory or Clinic is in a position to provide such facilities, maintain such equipment and standards as may be prescribed.

19. Certificate of registration:
    1. The Appropriate Authority shall, after holding an inquiry and after satisfying itself that the applicant has complied with all the requirements of this Act and the rules made thereunder and having regard to the advice of the Advisory Committee in this behalf, grant a certificate of registration in the prescribed form jointly or separately to the Genetic Counselling Centre, Genetic Laboratory or Genetic Clinic, as the case may be.
    2. If, after the inquiry and after giving an opportunity of being heard to the applicant and having regard to the advice of the Advisory Committee, the Appropriate Authority is satisfied that the applicant has not complied with the requirements of this Act or the rules, it shall, for reasons to be recorded in writing, reject the application for registration.
    3. Every certificate of registration shall be renewed in such manner and after such period and on payment of such fees as may be prescribed.
    4. The certificate of registration shall be displayed by the registered Genetic Counselling Centre, Genetic Laboratory or Genetic Clinic in a conspicuous place at its place of business.

20. Cancellation or suspension of registration:
    1. The Appropriate Authority may suo moto, or on complaint, issue a notice to the Genetic Counselling Centre, Genetic Laboratory or Genetic Clinic to show cause why its registration should not be suspended or cancelled for the reasons mentioned in the notice.
    2. If, after giving a reasonable opportunity of being heard to the Genetic Counselling Centre, Genetic

Laboratory or Genetic Clinic and having regard to the advice of the Advisory Committee, the Appropriate Authority is satisfied that there has been a breach of the provisions of this Act or the rules, it may, without prejudice to any criminal action that it may take against such Centre, Laboratory or Clinic, suspend its registration for such period as it may think fit or cancel its registration, as the case may be.

3. Notwithstanding anything contained in sub-sections (1) and (2), if the Appropriate Authority is, of the opinion that it is necessary or expedient so to do in the public interest, it may, for reasons to be recorded in writing, suspend the registration of any Genetic Counselling Centre, Genetic Laboratory or Genetic Clinic without issuing any such notice referred to in sub-section (1).

21. Appeal:

The Genetic Counselling Centre, Genetic Laboratory or Genetic Clinic may, within thirty days from the date of receipt of the order of suspension or cancellation of registration passed by the Appropriate Authority under section 20, prefer an appeal against such order to-

(i) the Central Government, where the appeal is against the order of the Central Appropriate Authority; and

(ii) the State Government, where the appeal is against the order of the State Appropriate Authority, in the prescribed manner.

Chapter VII
Offences and Penalties

22. Prohibition of advertisement relating to pre-natal determination of sex and punishment for contravention:

1. No person, organization, Genetic Counselling Centre, Genetic Laboratory or Genetic Clinic, including clinic, laboratory or centre having ultrasound machine or imaging machine or scanner or any other technology capable of undertaking determination of sex of foetus or sex selection shall issue,

publish, distribute, communicate or cause to be issued, published, distributed or communicated any advertisement, in any form, including internet, regarding facilities of pre-natal determination of sex or sex selection before conception available at such centre, laboratory, clinic or at any other place.

2. No person or organization including Genetic Counselling Centre, Genetic Laboratory or Genetic Clinic shall issue, publish, distribute, communicate or cause to be issued, published, distributed or communicated any advertisement in any manner regarding pre-natal determination or preconception selection of sex by any means whatsoever, scientific or otherwise.
3. Any person who contravenes the provisions of sub-section (1) or sub-section (2) shall be punishable with imprisonment for a term which may extend to three years and with fine which may extend to ten thousand rupees.

   Explanation: For the purposes of this section, "advertisement" includes any notice, circular, label, wrapper or any other document including advertisement through internet or any other media in electronic or print form and also includes any visible representation made by means of any hoarding, wall-painting, signal, light, sound, smoke or gas.

23. Offences and penalties:

    (1) Any medical geneticist, gynaecologist, registered medical practitioner or any person who owns a Genetic Counselling Centre, a Genetic Laboratory or a Genetic Clinic or is employed in such a Centre, Laboratory or Clinic and renders his professional or technical services to or at such a Centre, Laboratory or Clinic, whether on an honorary basis or otherwise, and who contravenes any of the provisions of this Act or rules made thereunder shall be punishable with imprisonment for a term which may

extend to three years and with fine which may extend to ten thousand rupees and on any subsequent conviction, with imprisonment which may extend to five years and with fine which may extend to fifty thousand rupees.

2. The name of the registered medical practitioner shall be reported by the Appropriate Authority to the State Medical Council concerned for taking necessary action including suspension of the registration if the charges are framed by the court and till the case is disposed of and on conviction for removal of his name from the register of the Council for a period of five years for the first offence and permanently for the subsequent offence.
3. Any person who seeks the aid of a Genetic Counselling Centre, Genetic Laboratory, Genetic Clinic or ultrasound clinic or imaging clinic or of a medical geneticist, gynaecologist, sonologist or imaging specialist or registered medical practitioner or any other person for sex selection or for conducting pre- natal diagnostic techniques on any pregnant women for the purposes other than those specified in sub-section (2) of section 4, he shall, be punishable with imprisonment for a term which may extend to three years and with fine which may extend to fifty thousand rupees for the first offence and for any subsequent offence with imprisonment which may extend to five years and with fine which may extend to one lakh rupees.
4. For the removal of doubts, it is hereby provided, that the provisions of sub-section (3) shall not apply to the woman who was compelled to undergo such diagnostic techniques or such selection.

24. Presumption in the case of conduct of pre-natal diagnostic techniques- Notwithstanding anything contained in the Indian Evidence Act, 1872, the court shall presume unless the contrary is proved that the pregnant woman was compelled by her husband or any other relative, as the case may be, to undergo pre-natal diagnostic

technique for the purposes other than those specified in sub-section (2) of section 4 and such person shall be liable for abetment of offence under sub-section (3) of section 23 and shall be punishable for the offence specified under that section.

25. Penalty for contravention of the provisions of the Act or rules for which no specific punishment is provided- Whoever contravenes any of the provisions of this Act or any rules made thereunder, for which no penalty has been elsewhere provided in this Act, shall be punishable with imprisonment for a term which may extend to three months or with fine, which may extend to one thousand rupees or with both and in the case of continuing contravention with an additional fine which may extend to five hundred rupees for every day during which such contravention continues after conviction for the first such contravention.

26. Offences by companies:

    1. Where any offence, punishable under this Act has been committed by a company, every person who, at the time the offence was committed was in charge of, and was responsible to the company for the conduct of the business of the company, as well as the company, shall be deemed to be guilty of the offence and shall be liable to be proceeded against and punished accordingly:

       Provided that nothing contained in this sub-section shall render any such person liable to any punishment, if he proves that the offence was committed without his knowledge or that he had exercised all due diligence to prevent the commission of such offence.

       Notwithstanding anything contained in sub-section (1), where any offence punishable under this Act has been committed by a company and it is proved that the offence has been committed with the consent or connivance of, or is attributable to any neglect on the part of, any director, manager, secretary or other officer of the company, such director, manager, secretary or other officer shall also be deemed to be guilty of that offence and shall be liable to be proceeded against and punished accordingly.

Explanation: For the purposes of this section-

(a) "company" means any body corporate and includes a firm or other association of individuals, and

(b) "director", in relation to a firm, means a partner in the firm.

27. Offence to be cognizable, non-bailable and non-compoundable: Every offence under this Act shall be cognizable, non-bailable and non-compoundable.

28. Cognizance of offences:

1. No court shall take cognizance of an offence under this Act except on a complaint made by

   (a) the Appropriate Authority concerned, or any officer authorised in this behalf by the Central Government or State Government, as the case may be, or the Appropriate Authority; or

   (b) a person who has given notice of not less than fifteen days in the manner prescribed, to the Appropriate Authority, of the alleged offence and of his intention to make a complaint to the court.

   Explanation: For the purpose of this clause, "person" includes a social organisation.

2. No court other than that of a Metropolitan Magistrate or a Judicial Magistrate of the first class shall try any offence punishable under this Act.

3. Where a complaint has been made under clause (b) of sub-section (1), the court may, on demand by such person, direct the Appropriate Authority to make available copies of the relevant records in its possession to such person.

Chapter VIII
Miscellaneous

29. Maintenance of records:

1. All records, charts, forms, reports, consent letters and all other documents required to be maintained under this Act and the rules shall be preserved for a period of two years or for such period as may be prescribed:
   Provided that, if any criminal or other proceedings are instituted against any Genetic Counselling Centre, Genetic Laboratory or Genetic Clinic, the records and all other documents of such Centre, Laboratory or Clinic shall be preserved till the final disposal of such proceedings.
2. All such records shall, at all reasonable times, be made available for inspection to the Appropriate Authority or to any other person authorised by the Appropriate Authority in this behalf.

30. Power to search and seize records, etc.:

1. If the Appropriate Authority has reason to believe that an offence under this Act has been or is being committed at any Genetic Counselling Centre, Genetic Laboratory or Genetic Clinic or any other place, such Authority or any officer authorised thereof in this behalf may, subject to such rules as may be prescribed, enter and search at all reasonable times with such assistance, if any, as such authority or officer considers necessary, such Genetic Counselling Centre, Genetic Laboratory or Genetic Clinic or any other place and examine any record, register, document, book, pamphlet, advertisement or any other material object found therein and seize and seal the same if such Authority or officer has reason to believe that it may furnish evidence of the commission of an office punishable under this Act.
2. The provisions of the Code of Criminal Procedure, 1973 (2 of 1974) relating to searches and seizures

shall, so far as may be, apply to every search or seizure made under this Act.

31. Protection of action taken in good faith: No suit, prosecution or other legal proceeding shall lie against the Central or the State Government or the Appropriate Authority or any officer authorised by the Central or State Government or by the Authority for anything which is in good faith, done or intended to be done in pursuance of the provisions of this Act.

31A. Removal of difficulties:

1. If any difficulty arises in giving effect to the provisions of the Pre-natal Diagnostic Techniques (Regulation and Prevention of Misuse) Amendment Act, 2002, the Central Government may, by order published in the Official Gazette, make such provisions not inconsistent with the provisions of the said Act as appear to it to be necessary or expedient for removing the difficulty.
   Provided that no order shall be made under this section after the expiry of a period of three years from the date of commencement of the Pre-natal Diagnostic Techniques (Regulation and Prevention of Misuse) Amendment Act, 2002.
2. Every order made under this section shall be laid, as soon as may be after it is made, before each House of Parliament.

32. Power to make rules:

1. The Central Government may make rules for carrying out the provisions of this Act.
2. In particular and without prejudice to the generality of the foregoing power, such rules may provide for-
   (i) the minimum qualifications for persons employed at a registered Genetic Counselling Centre, Genetic Laboratory or Genetic Clinic under clause (2) of section 3;
   (ia) the manner in which the person conducting ultrasonography on a pregnant woman shall

keep record thereof in the clinic under the proviso to sub-section (3) of section 4;

(ii) the form in which consent of a pregnant woman has to be obtained under section 5;

(iii) the procedure to be followed by the members of the Central Supervisory Board in the discharge of their functions under sub-section (4) of section 8;

(iv) allowances for members other than ex-officio members admissible under subsection (5) of section 9;

(iva) code of conduct to be observed by persons working at Genetic Counselling Centres, Genetic Laboratories and Genetic Clinics to be laid down by the Central Supervisory Board under clause (iv) of Section 16;

(ivb) the manner in which reports shall be furnished by the State and Union territory Supervisory Boards to the Board and the Central Government in respect of various activities undertaken in the State under the Act under clause (iv) of sub-section (1) of section 16A;

(ivc) empowering the Appropriate Authority in any other matter under clause (d) of section 17A;

(v) the period intervening between any two meetings of the Advisory Committee under the proviso to subsection (8) of section 17;

(vi) the terms and conditions subject to which a person may be appointed to the Advisory Committee and the procedure to be followed by such Committee under sub-section (9) of section 17;

(vii) the form and manner in which an application shall be made for registration and the fee payable thereof under sub-section (2) of section 18;

(viii) the facilities to be provided, equipment and other standards to be maintained by the Genetic

Counselling Centre, Genetic Laboratory or Genetic Clinic under sub-section (5) of section 18;

(ix) the form in which a certificate of registration shall be issued under sub-section (1) of section 19;

(x) the manner in which and the period after which a certificate of registration shall be renewed and the fee payable for such renewal under sub-section (3) of section 19;

(xi) the manner in which an appeal may be preferred under section 21;

(xii) the period up to which records, charts, etc., shall be preserved under sub-section (1) of section 29;

(xiii) the manner in which the seizure of documents, records, objects, etc., shall be made and the manner in which seizure list shall be prepared and delivered to the person from whose custody such documents, records or objects were seized under sub-section (1) of section 30;

(xiv) any other matter that is required to be, or may be, prescribed.

33. Power to make regulations: The Board may, with the previous sanction of the Central Government, by notification in the Official Gazette, make regulations not inconsistent with the provisions of this Act and the rules made thereunder to provide for

(a) the time and place of the meetings of the Board and the procedure to be followed for the transaction of business at such meetings and the number of members which shall form the quorum under sub-section (1) of section 9;

(b) the manner in which a person may be temporarily associated with the Board under sub-section (1) of section 11;

(c) the method of appointment, the conditions of service and the scales of pay and allowances of the officer and other employees of the Board appointed under section 12;

(d) generally for the efficient conduct of the affairs of the Board.

34. Rules and regulations to be laid before Parliament: Every rule and every regulation made under this Act shall be laid, as soon as may be after it is made, before each House of Parliament, while it is in session, for a total period of thirty days which may be comprised in one session or in two or more successive sessions, and if, before the expiry of the session immediately following the session or the successive sessions aforesaid, both Houses agree in making any modification in the rule or regulation or both Houses agree that the rule or regulation should not be made, the rule or regulation shall thereafter have effect only in such modified form or be of no effect, as the case may be; so, however, that any such modification or annulment shall be without prejudice to the validity of anything previously done under that rule or regulation.

Bibliography

Allan, B.B., R. Brant, J. Seidel and J.F. Jarrel. 1997. 'Declining Sex Ratio in Canada'. *Canad Med Ass J*, 156: 37–41.

Andersson, R. and S. Bergstrom. 1998. 'Is Maternal Malnutrition Associated with a Low Sex Ratio at Birth?'. *Human Biology*, December, 70(6): 1, 101–6.

Astolfi, P. and L.A. Zonta. 1999. 'Reduced Male Births in Major Italian Cities'. *Hum Reprod*, 14: 3116–9.

Bartels, I., I. Hansmann and B. Eiben. 1990. 'Excess of Females in Chromosomally Normal Spontaneous Abortuses'. *Am J Med Genet*, 35: 297–8.

Biggar, R.J., J. Wohlfahrt, T. Westergaard and M. Melbye. 1999. 'Sex Ratios, Family Size, and Birth Order'. *American Journal of Epidemiology*, November 1, 150(9): 957–62.

Bromen, K. and K.H. Jockel. 1997. 'Change in Male Proportion among Newborn Infants'. *Lancet*, 349: 805–6.

Chahnazarian, A. 1988. 'Determinants of the Sex Ratio at Birth: Review of Recent Literature'. *Social Biology*, Fall-Winter, 35(3–4): 214–35.

Chen, L.C. 1982. 'Where have the Women Gone? Insights from Bangladesh on Low Sex Ratio of India's Population'. *Economic and Political Weekly*, March 6, 17(10): 364–72.

Choe, M.K., H. Hao and F. Wang. 1995. 'Effects of Gender, Birth Order, and Other Correlates on Childhood Mortality in China'. *Social Biology*, Spring-Summer, 42(1–2): 50–64.

D'Souza, V.S. 1994. 'Declining Sex Ratio and the Demographic Transition in India', in K.B. Pathak, U.P. Sinha and Arvind Pandey (eds), *Dynamics of Population and Family Welfare*, Bombay, Himalaya Publishing House, pp. 305–21.

George, S.M. and R.S. Dahiya. 1998. 'Female Foeticide in Rural Haryana'. *Economic and Political Weekly*, August 8–14, 33(32): 2, 191–8.

Ghosh, S. 1990. 'Discrimination against the Female Child'. *Indian Journal of Maternal and Child Health*, October–December, 1(4): 104–8.

Goswami, Sambodh. 2007. *Female Infanticide and Child Marriage*. Jaipur: Rawat Publications.

Guerrero, R. 1975. 'Type and Time of Insemination within the Menstrual Cycle and the Human Sex Ratio at Birth'. *Studies in Family Planning*, October, 6(10): 367–71.

James, W.H. 1996. 'Male Reproductive Hazards and Occupation'. *Lancet*, 347: 773.

—. 1995. 'What Stabilizes the Sex Ratio?'. *Annals of Human Genetics*, April, 59(2): 243–9.

Karkal, M. and S. Ghogale. 1976. 'On the Determinants of Sex of a Child within a Family', in M. Karkal, J. Kumar and T.K. Roy (eds), *Sex Ratio: Demographic Analysis*, Bombay: International Institute for Population Studies, pp. 73–81.

Lowe, C.R. and T. Mckeown. 1950. 'The Sex Ratio of Human Births Related to Maternal Age'. *British Journal of Social Medicine*, 4: 75–85.

Markle, G.E. 1974. 'Sex Ratio at Birth: Values, Variance, and Some Determinants'. *Demography*, February, 11(1): 131–42.

Martin, J.F. 1995. 'Hormonal and Behavioral Determinants of the Secondary Sex Ratio'. *Social Biology*, Fall-Winter, 42(3–4): 226–38.

Miller, B. 1981. *The Endangered Sex: The Neglect of Female Children in Rural India*. Ithaca, NY: Cornell University Press.

—. 1985. 'Prenatal and Postnatal Sex-selection in India: The Patriarchal Context, Ethical Questions and Public Policy', *Working Paper No. 107*, Lansing, Mich.: Michigan State University.

Mocarelli, P., P. Brambilla, P.M. Gerthoux, D.G. Patterson and L.L. Needham. 1996. 'Change in Sex Ratio with Exposure to Dioxin'. *Lancet*, 348: 409.

Mulder, M.B. 1994. 'On Polygyny and Sex Ratio at Birth: An Evaluation of Whiting's Study'. *Current Anthropology*, December, 35(5): 625–7.

Oechsli, F.W. 1974. 'Oral Contraception and Sex Ratio at Birth'. *Lancet*, May 18, 1(7864): 1004–5.

Pakrasi, K. and A. Halder. 1971. 'Sex Ratios and Sex Sequences of Births in India'. *Journal of Biosocial Science*, 3: 377–87.

Pohlman, E. 1968. 'Some Effects of Being Able to Control Sex of Offspring'. *Eugenics Quarterly*, 14(4): 274–81.

Prakasam, C.P. and V.S. Sastry. 1983. 'The Influence of Birth Order, Maternal Age on Sex Ratio at Birth in Greater Bombay'. *Janasamkhya*, June, 1(1): 75–83.

Rajani Kumari, J. and T. Venkateswar Rao. 1982. 'Seasonal Variation of Human Sex Ratio at Birth and the Modifying Factors'. *Indian Journal of Pediatrics*, July–August, 49(399): 541–6.

Ramachandran, K.V. and V.A. Deshpande. 1964. 'The Sex Ratio at Birth in India by Regions'. *Milbank Memorial Fund Quarterly*, 42(2): 84–94.

Rubin, E. 1967. 'The Sex Ratio at Birth'. *American Statistician*, October, 21(4): 45–8.

Russell, W.T. 1936. 'Statistical Study of the Sex Ratio at Birth'. *Journal of Hygiene*, 36: 381–401.

Sachar, R.K., J. Verma, V. Prakash, A. Chopra, R. Adlaka and R. Sofat. 1990. 'Sex Selective Fertility Control: An Outrage'. *Journal of Family Welfare*, June, 36(2): 30–5.

Sachar, R.K., R. Sehgal, J. Verma, V. Prakash and W.P. Singh. 1990. 'The Female Child: A Picture of Denials and Deprivations'. *Indian Journal of Maternal and Child Health*, October–December, 1(4): 124–6.

Sehgal, R., R.K. Sachar, J. Verma, V. Prakash, A. Goyal and R.K. Soni. 1990. 'Unwanted, Unwelcome and Unborn: The Female Foetus'. *Indian Journal of Maternal and Child Health*, October–December, 1(4): 144–5.

Sekher, T.V. and Neelambar Hatti (eds). 2010. *Unwanted Daughters: Gender Discrimination in Modern India*. Jaipur: Rawat Publications.

Shaw, C. 1989. 'The Sex Ratio at Birth in England and Wales'. *Population Trends*, Autumn, 57: 26–9.

She, W. 1996. 'Selective Sex Identification of Foetus Banned'. *China Population Today*, June, 13(3): 15.

Srivastava, M.L. and A.K. Sinha. 1975. 'Sex Sequences of Births in India'. *Journal of Biosocial Science*, July, 7(3): 233–41.

Strobino, B., J. Kline and D. Warburton. 1988. 'Spermicide Use and Pregnancy Outcome'. *American Journal of Public Health*, March, 78(3): 260–3.

Sudha, S. and S.I. Rajan. 1999. 'Female Demographic Disadvantage in India 1981–1991: Sex Selective Abortions and Female Infanticide'. *Development and Change*, July, 30(3): 585–618.

Vartiainen, T., L. Kartovaara and J. Tuomisto. 1999. 'Environmental Chemicals and Changes in Sex Ratio: Analysis Over 250 Years in Finland'. *Environ Health Perspect*, 107: 813–5.

Williams, R.J. and S.P. Gloster. 1992. 'Human Sex Ratio as it Relates to Caloric Availability'. *Social Biology*, Fall-Winter, 39(3–4): 285–91.

Index